Shadows of the Civil War

SHADOWS OF THE CIVIL WAR

D. Quinn MIlls

MindEdge Press
Waltham, Massachusetts

ISBN: 0977062678
ISBN-13: 978-0-9770626-7-6

MindEdge Press
Waltham, Massachusetts

Printed in the United States

CONTENTS

INTRODUCTION

"The past is never dead. It's not even past." – William Faulkner

The American Civil War ended almost 150 years ago, yet its shadows hang over our country to this day. The war accomplished two very good things—it kept the nation together and it ended slavery—but it left a residue of resentments, fears, brutalities and hypocrisies. This residue is very important in American life today, and includes shadows that need to be lifted.

The Civil War was the greatest conflict Americans have ever fought; it cost us more lives in both absolute and relative terms than any other war. It is a war that left one of its prime purposes incompletely resolved—for it freed the slaves but did not provide economic opportunity to them. It is also our only war that victimized much of our civilian population. It left a third of our country impoverished for a century. We do not realize how deeply this war seared our national personality and forged our character. The impact was good and bad. We are all familiar with the good. It is time after a century and a half to recognize the bad and try to put it behind us.

PART ONE

The Civil War Defined America

CHAPTER ONE

Today's America Began in Our Civil War

Many of the key elements of our national character emerged in the Civil War and continue today.

The American Civil War ended a century and a half ago. Yet there remains widespread interest in it. Why?

One cause is the continuing engagement of Civil War buffs—people who find the narrative of the war fascinating. These are people who are intrigued by the events, personalities and drama of the war.

But there is more to the continuing significance of the Civil War than historical interest. In particular, the Civil War saw the nation divide into sections in a way that continues to strongly define our politics. The most significant element of American national politics today is the continuing sectional divide in our presidential elections. Today each major political party starts a presidential election with a strong base in a section of the country—and the election is decided by voters in a few states which are called "swing" states, which might go either way in the election. This is a direct legacy of the Civil War.

There is much mythology about the significance of the period of the Civil War and Reconstruction in today's America. Media, most commentators and even historians of the Civil War period pretend that the nation is essentially uniform, as if there were no separate development or history of the sections. In discussions of contemporary elections, for example, Illinois and Georgia are treated as if they were both part of the same whole with only minor differences—in the same way that members of a family are mostly alike but with some different features that generally do not conceal the underlying commonality of the family.

Yet the sectional division in American politics is obvious from maps of recent election results. It is ignored by both major political parties—even to the point of denial. Democrats benefit from this practice because it conceals the limited base in the Northeast and Far West from which they operate. Republicans benefit from the practice because it conceals their current ties to the unpopular social attitudes of the Southern past. Thus, for their own very different reasons, both liberals and conservatives today pretend that the nation is more homogenous than it is. Neither position is convincing because both ignore the facts.

This is one of the most powerful and pervasive myths of American politics—held to firmly by both left and right. The myth is that the United States is a compact—expressed in the Constitution—freely made and freely adhered to by all its people.

It is more accurate to say that the United States began its current existence at the end of the Civil War than to say that it began at the time of the Revolution. The original compact was dissolved practically if not by law in 1861. Another quite different arrangement was established by war and military occupation of the Southern states over the 15 years ending in 1876. There were five years of vigorous war and ten years of military occupation of the South to establish today's nation.

Another very important reason for continuing interest in the Civil War—though probably the reason least recognized by the American population—is that the issues and outcomes of the Civil War remain at the heart of American politics today.

Beneath the sectional divide in present-day American national politics lie the strong emotions underlying the Civil War. The issues over which it was fought continue to fester in Americans today. The war ended slavery, but it left us with a heritage of racism. For example, a recent controversy involves the question whether or not it is discriminatory against African-American military personnel for them to be assigned to serve at military bases named for Confederate generals. Another controversy involves whether or not the names of Harvard alumni who were Confederate soldiers should be listed in the university's Memorial Hall along with Harvard alumni who were Union soldiers.

There have been many changes in America since the Civil War, and the War has played little role in a great many of them. In some things the legacy of the War is considerable; in others, it has no role at all.

In some areas the influence of the Civil War is both great and unfortunate. These include, for example, the residential segregation of our population by race; the continuing economic lagging of the African-American community; the way we think about and wage war; and a predilection to see conflict always in moral terms with a resultant propensity to hypocrisy.

Racism is the most recognized and discussed residue of the Civil War. This is because the War ended slavery but not racism. But other legacies are also very important. For example, America's tradition of waging war against the civilian populations of opponents also has its origins in the Civil War.

It is useful, therefore, to call attention to the continuing legacy of the War and to ask the question: Will we ever be free of the shadows of the American Civil War?

CHAPTER TWO

How America Divided Sectionally

The Civil War found us and left us a divided nation.

The Origin of the United States

The Declaration of Independence states that "all men are created equal." This seems to some critics a monumental expression of hypocrisy because many of its signers owned slaves and most of them harbored attitudes that we would today describe as racist. Yet the Declaration's endorsement of human rights was made possible without its signers' utter hypocrisy because they believed that slavery was non-economical and on its way to extinction. If this were the case, then the challenge of slavery to the idealism of the Declaration of Independence could be expected to disappear over a few ensuing decades.

In the aftermath of the Revolution, the United States was cobbled together as a single nation by a group of compromises. In part, these compromises bridged gaps between the southern and northern states. For example, the South demanded that slaves be counted for Congressional representation, although they could not vote. Northerners rejected the notion. The resultant compromise was that each slave would count as two-thirds of a person for Congressional representation. Slavery was thereby explicitly recognized by the Constitution. Abolitionists—a small minority at the time of the adoption of the Constitution—opposed this.

The federal government was given limited powers. Many people presumed that the individual states were the primary seats of power. During the War of 1812 with Great Britain, the New England states asserted a right to leave the Union when federal policy damaged their interests. At the time, Southern and mid-Atlantic states controlled the federal government and pursued policies unfavorable to New England.

Over the first decades of the nation's life processes of centralization occurred. The Supreme Court asserted jurisdiction over state courts and the right to determine the powers of the federal and state governments.

Population growth was more rapid in the Northern states than in the South. Senators and Congresspersons from newly created Midwestern states joined in voting with the Northeastern states so that the South began to see itself as a permanent minority in the national government. The South began to seek limitation on the power of the majority. As part of this effort, the South picked up New England's earlier assertion of a right of secession and voiced it with increasing vigor.

In the first decades of the nation deep divisions emerged between the South and the North. They were economic, social and political. The North began to industrialize and sought federal government help in building an infrastructure of canals, roads and ports to facilitate trade within and outside of the United States. Further, the Northern states insisted on tariffs on manufactured goods imported to the United States from abroad—thus providing financial protection to the growing Northern manufacturing interests. The South remained primarily agrarian and opposed Northern-sponsored public works and tariffs. The South wished to purchase manufactured goods as cheaply as possible from abroad—that is, without tariffs; and the South resented having to pay in part for infrastructure improvements which benefited the North primarily.

Thus, the initial divisions between South and North were primarily economic.

The Emerging Significance of Slavery

There were debates in Congress even before the turn of the 19th century about slavery. Some Northern legislators attacked the institution and some Southern legislators defended it. The debate aired the major arguments that were to be presented by both North and South decades later when the issue of slavery became a cause of disruption of the Union. But after the first outburst of tension over slavery, the issue subsided for decades in Congress.

There is controversy about the cause of this. Some historians argue that the topic of slavery was so divisive—even in the late 18th century—that it had to be swept under the rug in order for the United States to get started at all. For pragmatic political reasons, therefore, slavery became the issue that could not be discussed; the elephant in the room that all pretended not to see.

Yet it is possible that this interpretation is an extrapolation of the future controversy over slavery into the past. That is, we know today that the slavery issue was to have a key role in the Civil War. We know that the abolition of slavery was a major consequence of the War. Hence, it is easy to project the importance of slavery into the past. So, goes this line of thought, if the United States were at that time not openly obsessed with slavery, then it must be because the country was hiding its obsession.

But this seems to some to be exactly the kind of projection of the future onto the past that responsible historians continually denounce.

An alternative view is that slavery was not much discussed for the first three decades of the existence of the United States for two reasons. First, discussion of slavery was muted because Northern interests were profiting from slavery. The pre-Civil War period saw two levels of exploitation—the exploitation of slaves by planters, and of planters by banks and other forms of lenders. Since, of course, major banks were Northern, the North played an indirect role in the exploitation of slaves, gaining economically by it. Northerners had also been involved in the slave trade. So both by slave trading and financial lending the North was benefiting from slavery. There was reluctance in the North to end a good thing financially. Over time, moral outrage over slavery in the North pushed economic interests into the background. Further, the North was beginning to industrialize. New economic interests were displacing the old ones which had benefited from slavery.

Second, slavery did not dominate the public agenda in the early years of the Republic because slavery was not thought to be that important. Other issues dominated the national political agenda and were fought out in elections and legislatively with great vigor on all sides. Perhaps slavery was on its way to extinction because of economic disadvantages. Tobacco was grown by slaves in Virginia, but as the land became exhausted, growing tobacco with slaves was becoming too expensive to be profitable. Rice was grown with slaves in South Carolina and Georgia, but mid-western wheat was displacing rice as a food in America. Cotton was grown in most Southern states, but it was so laborious to grow and harvest that it had only a limited market. Hence, slave-worked agriculture was not prospering and it was possible to envision its peaceful extinction. It was this expectation that had made the Declaration of Independence somewhat less than pure hypocrisy.

But after the American Revolution in 1794 Eli Whitney patented the cotton gin, a device which made cotton grown by slave labor on Southern plantations greatly profitable. New cotton-growing states were settled and brought into the Union—Alabama, Mississippi, Tennessee, and Arkansas—the so-called Deep South. In Virginia where slaves had grown tobacco, slavery continued to experience economic decline. In the Carolinas and Georgia, where slaves had cultivated rice, cotton became a major crop. In the new states of the Deep South, cotton was the principal crop. There grew up in the South a new economy based on cotton and slavery. It became obvious that slavery was now profitable again in many Southern states and was not going to disappear because of adverse economic conditions.

Meanwhile, the Midwest was also being settled, largely by farmers who grew food crops. Much Midwestern produce was shipped down the Mississippi River to New Orleans and thence to final consumers in the United States or abroad. But the construction of a transportation infrastructure of canals and railways also permitted shipment of agricultural produce to the Northeast. The South and the Northeast began to compete for the receipt and transshipment of Midwestern produce.

The sectional division of the United States was now clear: the South vied with the Northeast for economic and political advantage and the Midwestern states were sought-after by the two other sections.

Meanwhile, there grew up in the English-speaking world a movement—largely originating in the Protestant churches—for the abolition of the slave trade and then of slavery itself. The first major success was the abolition of the slave trade —the importation to the Americas of slaves from Africa. This was largely accomplished by the British, who had command of the seas. The reformers then turned to the abolition of slavery itself. A growing abolitionist movement developed in New England.

By the end of the second decade of the 19th century the sectional divide in American politics was a dominant concern. The issues included the tariff, federal support for infrastructure improvements, the extension of slavery to federal territories and new states, and the property rights, if any, of slaveholders resident or visiting in the non-Southern states. Increasingly bitter political disputes led to a series of compromises which were never able to fully settle the issues. Abolitionist agitation grew stronger.

In 1856 a new political party, the Republicans, ran a candidate for president. The party failed to win the election, but it endorsed the political agenda of the Northeastern states which included restriction of slavery to the southern states and its exclusion from the new states in the west and southwest.

Under increasing political pressure from abolitionists, Southerners became increasingly resentful. People began to talk openly of disunion.

The Crisis that Led to the American Civil War

The presidential election of 1860 saw the Democratic Party offer three different candidates to oppose the single candidate of the Republican Party. With the Democratic vote divided three ways, the Republican candidate won the election by a plurality of the popular vote. The newly elected President of the United States, Abraham Lincoln, won 18 of 29 states but less than 40 percent of the popular vote. It is useful to remember when considering the somewhat extreme methods used by the Lincoln Administration in winning the Civil War that Lincoln never received a majority of the popular vote of all American citizens in either of his Presidential victories (recalling that Lincoln always insisted that potential voters in the Southern states during the war were actually still citizens of the United States, even if not willing, able nor entitled to vote in the second presidential election which Lincoln won).

The immediate crisis that led to war had its origins in the reassertion by several Southern states of a supposed right of each state to leave the Union if it desired. A group of states decided to secede from the United States and took legislative action to do so. They elected a president, Jefferson Davis of Mississippi, and formed an army.

President-elect Lincoln insisted that there was no right of any state to leave the Union. "They," he said of the Southern leadership, "have no obligation to leave the Union, while I have taken a most sacred oath to preserve it." Lincoln was referring to the oath he took at his inauguration as President in which he swore to uphold and defend the Constitution of the United States. In his interpretation, the Constitution did not permit any state to secede from the Union.

Lincoln called up volunteers for an army to compel the seceding states to remain in the Union. This precipitated the secession of several more states. The 11 states that seceded then formed a loose association of states calling itself the Confederate States of America.

As these events transpired, it became apparent that the most effective political forces in North and South were preparing for war. The North elected Lincoln to the presidency and thereby provoked the South; the South left the Union in a fit of anger as a result. The country split apart.

South Carolina began the war by attacking a federal garrison at Fort Sumter in Charleston harbor on April 12, 1861.

Measures of Potential Power

The two sides were not evenly matched. The 11 states of the Confederacy had a population of some nine million people, about four million of whom were slaves. The North had a population of some 22 million of whom very few were slaves. Using the rule of thumb that a nation's manpower potential for war is one-sixth of its population, the North could call more than 3.6 million men to its colors while the South, unwilling to try to enlist slaves in its army, could call only some 800,000. The North therefore had a manpower advantage of some four and one-half times that of the South.

To make the disparity even greater, the North was able to call upon slaves of the South who were freed during the War to serve in its armies. Thus, as the war continued, the manpower advantage of the North increased. Adding the potential military manpower of the slave population to the North's own military manpower meant that the North had a manpower advantage over the South of almost five and one-half times.

Finally, during the War immigration from Europe, especially from Ireland, continued at a rapid pace. Many of the immigrants were men of military age, and many were drafted directly into the Union Army. Another several hundred thousand men were thereby added to the manpower potential of the Union. In total, the Union advantage in manpower potential over the South was six to one.

The North also had most of the manufacturing and industrial capacity of the nation. It also possessed a much more extensive railway network than the South, enabling it to move soldiers and supplies much more effectively. The North had financial strength that the South lacked; it held the national capital of Washington, D. C., and the North had the military forces of the national government which were in existence at the time the conflict commenced.

Though it was at a serious disadvantage in terms of population, economic resources and military strength, the South had certain advantages. It had an extensive territory which the North was required to conquer if the North were to force the South to reenter the Union; it had a deeply indented coastline which would be hard for the North to blockade; it had high civilian morale; it had some excellent military leadership; and it had the possibility of support from major foreign powers, especially Britain and France, each of which wished to see the United States weakened.

As war impended, many Southerners left service with the military forces of the United States and entered those of the Confederacy.

The War

The Civil War was the most costly in human terms of any war ever fought by the United States. The dead appear to have numbered more than three-quarters of a million—more than twice the number of dead in the next largest American war, World War II. The Civil War was fought for four years over much of the southern United States.

The first year of the war (1861) involved confused battles as the two sides organized their armies and leadership. The second year (1862) saw major Union offenses in Virginia in the east and in Kentucky and Tennessee in the west. Both Union offenses were blunted by Confederate responses. In the east the Confederates won a series of victories; in the west Union successes were dissipated by a failure to coordinate the actions of various Union forces.

The first two years of the war saw six major developments. First, the Union won control of the Border States—Missouri, Kentucky, and Maryland—except Virginia, which is not ordinarily considered a border state but which geographically and politically was one. In

Virginia the North won control of the western counties which were to become the state of West Virginia.

There was a strong party of Southern sympathizers in each of the Border States. Lincoln recognized that the conflict would be lost by the North if the Border States joined the Confederacy. By military and political means Lincoln contrived to keep the Border States in the Union and made possible, thereby, the North's ultimate victory. Control of the Border States was key to the Union's eventual military victory, for it opened the middle southern states (Tennessee, Mississippi, Alabama and Georgia) to invasion. Union control of the Border States also prevented the southern states from having a critical mass of population and territory which the Union would have been unlikely to have been able to conquer.

Second, the Lincoln Administration demonstrated that it could contain strong political sentiment in the Union states for peace with the South. The challenge was significant. "Let us allow our erring sister states to depart in peace," one peace advocate urged. By continual attention to the politics of the Union states; by jailing the war's political opponents; and by effective media communications and propaganda, Lincoln kept the war effort going.

Third, the Lincoln Administration was able to persuade the major European powers that they should not recognize the Confederacy as an independent nation, thereby denying the Confederacy what might have been decisive support in the war.

Fourth, the Union drew a naval blockade around the southern states which strangled the South financially and militarily—the South was unable to export its cotton and unable to acquire needed weapons abroad.

Fifth, recognizing the enormous human, material and financial cost that the war was imposing on the North, Lincoln sought to enhance political support by embracing a moral objective—the abolition of slavery in the United States.

Sixth, there appeared in both Confederate and Union forces remarkable military leadership. For the South, Robert E. Lee began a series of victories over superior Union forces which prolonged the war. For the North, Ulysses Simpson Grant and William Tecumseh Sherman emerged as the team that would eventually win the war.

The middle year of the war, 1863, saw its decisive moments. Lee overreached by invading Pennsylvania and attempting to destroy the major Union army at Gettysburg. The defeat of Lee's army ended Southern offensives in the east. In the west Grant seized the Confederate fortress at Vicksburg which had blocked Union shipping on the Mississippi. By capturing Vicksburg Grant split the Confederacy in half, severing its eastern two-thirds from the remainder which was west of the Mississippi (Louisiana, Arkansas, and Texas).

Despite decisive defeats at Gettysburg and Vicksburg the South continued the war for another two years in the hope that the North would tire of the fighting and make peace. That is, the South for the final two years of the war hoped for a political victory rather than a military victory.

Throughout the war the South's objective was its separation from the United States. No significant effort was ever made or contemplated by the Confederate government to conquer any or all of the Northern states. In contrast, the effort of the North from the beginning was to suppress the rebellion of the southern states by occupying Southern territory.

The final two years of the war were spent by the North in subduing the South. A critical point was reached in the fall of 1864 when Lincoln stood for re-election as president. In the summer of that year it appeared that Lincoln was likely to lose re-election. Lincoln had significant opposition from Democrats in the North who wanted an end to the war. The war itself had dragged on another full year after the great Union victories at Gettysburg and Vicksburg. It seemed that the Lincoln Administration could not bring the conflict to an end. The cost in human lives and material was continually rising.

But in the late summer of 1864 Sherman seized Atlanta and it became clear to all that the war would come to an end at some point with a Union victory. Lincoln won re-election and the fate of the South was sealed.

Yet another six months were required by the Union to complete its conquest of the South. Sherman took his army through Georgia and South Carolina, devastating the country and burning cities as he went. Grant pressed his siege of Lee's army south of the Southern capital of Richmond, Virginia. The great military difference of the last year of the war was that Union armies in the west and east were finally cooperating in one overall strategic plan for destroying the ability of the South to resist militarily. By the spring of 1865 Sherman's army of the west had moved to the Carolinas and was approaching Grant's army from the south. Lee's army was trapped between the two.

In April, 1865, Lee surrendered his army, and within two months resistance had ceased in the Southern states. The political leaders of the Confederacy were captured soon thereafter by Union forces.

The war was over.

Political Reconstruction in the South

The war ended and there began a period of political upheaval. Lincoln had always maintained that the Southern states had never legally left the Union because there was no right of secession. Hence, as the various Southern states were conquered by Union forces, Lincoln permitted them to return to their participation in the political life of the nation under leadership that had in many instances been supportive of the Confederacy.

But Lincoln was assassinated at the moment of Union victory. His successor, Andrew Johnson, tried to continue Lincoln's approach to the reintegration of the South into the nation's political life. But influential Northern politicians and many of their constituents took a very different view. First, they felt that the rebellious Southerners should pay for the bloodshed and destruction caused by the war. Second, they were infuriated by what they saw as mistreatment economically, socially and politically in the South of freed slaves.

Finally, they saw the balance of power in the nation shifting away from them when Southern legislators reentered Congress, and they wished to preserve their control of the national government.

There followed a series of laws that disenfranchised white Southerners and put Northern immigrants (so-called "carpet-baggers" from the luggage they carried) and freed slaves in control of state governments in the South. This was the period of Reconstruction. It ended in 1877, having consumed a period double in length to that of the war itself.

To win the disputed presidential election of 1876 the Republicans surrendered nationally-imposed political control in the Southern states. Some isolated pockets of federally-imposed political control continued for a further period, but the process of Reconstruction was essentially ended at that time. Soon all Southern states were again in the political control of the people who had led secession and the war effort. Former slaves were disenfranchised and segregated from the white population by what were labeled "Jim Crow" laws.

Almost 100 years later, in part as a consequence of the Civil Rights Movement, Jim Crow laws were outlawed, African-Americans were enfranchised, and segregation of public facilities was outlawed. De jure ("by law") segregation was ended in the United States. De facto segregation of residential areas and many private institutions continues to this day in both North and South.

The Sectional Consequences of the Civil War

The great political and military conflict between North and South absorbed much of the domestic history of the United States from roughly 1820 (the negotiation of the Missouri Compromise) until 1965 (the passage of the Voting Rights Act). The war did not create the sectional division of the nation—it had existed from the nation's inception. But until the Civil War the sectional division was merely a political rivalry, and the country functioned as a representative democracy with a majority ruling subject to the checks and balances of the Constitution. The Civil War changed that.

The Civil War thus turned a sectional orientation into a sectional fault line. Sectionalism became a great chasm in American politics which remains today.

The war left the Southern states impoverished for a century. In the America that emerged from the war the South was a poverty-stricken and bitter section, largely concealing its resentment for fear of Northern retaliation, but always on the other side of the Northeast politically. The Northeast was left in general direction of our national economy and our national politics through today. Had the war turned out differently, everything of importance in American political, social and economic life would be different. A substantial minority of Americans—the white Southerners—did everything they could to make that different America a reality. That they failed is a defining fact in American history.

CHAPTER THREE

The War Decided Much: It Preserved the Union and Ended Slavery

It is sometimes asserted that wars do not settle anything; that military conflict is always a waste of lives and resources. But the American Civil War settled much—it ended slavery in the United States and forced political unification.

The Union Preserved

The victory of the North in the Civil War was so complete that the country was thereafter reunified to a significant degree and has acted as one in subsequent wars. Former Confederate officers played a constructive role in American military history. Former Confederate politicians served the United States. Their descendants did also. Citizens of the former Confederate states were loyal to the United States. The political issues of the war were settled. No significant attempt has been made to secede again or to restore chattel slavery.

In part, this was due to the completeness of the Union military victory, but that's not all there was to it. Union politicians and military leaders were concerned as the war ended that a guerilla campaign would be started against the Union forces that might last for years and render Union victory incomplete. In part in an attempt to avoid this, victorious Union leaders imposed relatively lenient terms of surrender on Confederate forces.

In early April, 1865, Lee's army was surrounded. Lee surrendered to Grant at Appomattox Court House. Grant offered magnanimous terms of surrender. Lee resisted urgings from some of his officers to point his troops toward the continuation of the war by guerilla means. Instead, he set an example of abandoning the struggle completely. In a few weeks all Confederate forces had surrendered. Jefferson Davis, the President of the Confederacy, fled into Georgia attempting to reach Mexico, but was captured about a month after Lee's surrender. He was imprisoned in Virginia. There was a vigorous controversy in the North about his treatment. Many wanted him tried and executed for treason against the United States because he had waged war against the United States for four years. But he was neither tried nor punished severely. His wife was allowed to join him in prison, and after two years he was released on bail. He lived for 24 years after the end of the war, even paying an amicable visit to former President Ulysses S. Grant in New York City when Grant was dying. Nor was Lee tried for treason and punished. Instead, he became president of a college in Virginia and died five years after the end of the war.

The lenient treatment of the Southern leaders after the war did much to reconcile the South to its forcible re-inclusion in the United States. At the end of the Civil War, Southern leadership gave examples of accepting with good grace the determination of the battlefield.

But it is easy to exaggerate the degree to which the wounds of the war were healed afterwards and have healed even today. The counsels of acceptance of defeat by the Southern leadership were not a repentance of their attempt at separation. Nor were these gestures by the Southern leadership evidence of reconciliation, as the North likes to pretend. They were merely acquiescence in a disliked reality. Southern leadership never apologized for its attempt to gain independence. They regretted not secession, but defeat – that is, they regretted losing the war. And that remains the opinion of most Southerners today, though in today's period of thought coercion via political correctness many will not divulge it to others. If they do, they will be denounced and abused in public by Northerners both liberal and conservative.

Slavery's Residue of Racism Has Slowly Declined since the War

Overtime, Southerners and Northerners alike have come to reject not only slavery but, to a lesser degree, racism. Slavery and racism were great evils, and the first is now gone in America and the second seems in decline. Many, if not most, Southerners now recognize that the effort to preserve slavery and racism was a moral error. These are unambiguous gains from the Civil War and its aftermath.

Examples are not hard to find. Southerners today have very different attitudes about race than did their ancestors. Not long ago a man died in South Carolina where he had lived all his life. He was from a wealthy family which had long ago owned slaves. He was very old fashioned and a bigot. In a eulogy his best friend commented on how shocked the old man must have been by how he died. He was hit by a car in Charleston on Martin Luther King Boulevard. The notion of a major avenue in Charleston that was named for an African-American civil rights leader must have been very difficult for the old man to accept.

A Unified Economy Was Maintained

The economic strength of the United States since the Civil War owes much to the unity imposed by the Civil War. If the South had been successful in dividing the nation, then we'd now have economic fragmentation. There would be impediments to trade between North and South. There would probably be tariff and non-tariff barriers to trade and the sorts of proceedings that occur under the General Agreement on Trade and Tariffs (GATT). The South might have remained much more agrarian than it is today, so that the diverse economy which now exists in our geographic sections would not exist. This would leave us two much weaker economies than the merged and diversified economy which we have today. Two sovereign nations would divide the center of North America and the parts would likely be much less than their potential sum.

In the Confederacy there would likely be trade barriers between the states. This is because the Confederacy was formed by states peculiarly protective of their sovereignty— that's the very reason for their leaving the United States, in their view. Secession was to enforce the rights of the states against any central governmental authority. The Confederacy struggled throughout the war to have enough central power to prosecute the conflict successfully against the relatively centralized north. It failed.

Even today, with the Union fully in place and national law protecting free commerce among the states (via the Commerce clause of the Constitution), some states find devious ways to erect barriers to commerce. For example, most automobile and truck drivers to and from Florida must pass through Georgia. Georgia is prohibited by the federal Constitution from placing tolls on travelers in transit. So instead Georgia utilizes the subterfuge of its police power. Georgia police routinely stop motorists in transit for alleged (and often actual) speeding violations and levy substantial fees on them—hundreds of dollars. These are a disguised toll on motorists. Had the Confederacy survived the war, Georgia would probably have retained the authority under the constitution of the Confederacy to levy tolls directly with an enhanced negative impact on interstate commerce in the South. There might even have been tariffs and other barriers to trade among the states of the Confederacy.

Hence, Union victory in the war preserved a unified national marketplace created by severely restricting each state's interference with interstate commerce. This helped lay the foundations for economic growth in America after the Civil War and helps preserve a strong economy today.

CHAPTER FOUR

The History and Meaning of the Civil War Are Subject to Very Different Treatments Today

Different political factions today stress different interpretations of the War. They do this for their own political advantage and to reinforce their convictions. To avoid being misled by current political commentary about the Civil War, we must try to keep an open mind as we consider its shadows.

A Hot Political Topic

There is no other part of American history that gets as much current attention as the Civil War. The Revolution founded our nation, but it gets little attention except from the conservatives in our political spectrum. The period of the 1930s between World Wars I and II is pointed to when either or both political parties want to argue for military intervention in some other countries (most recently, Syria and Ukraine). The argument is that early intervention could prevent a much more difficult struggle later—in the way that World War II might have been avoided if we had intervened against Hitler's Germany early in its existence. But references to the interwar years are made primarily for this purpose; otherwise the 1930s are remembered only for the Great Depression—something we reference infrequently, hoping to avoid repetition of it. World War II was the most recent of our great wars, but it is almost ignored in our political discussions.

In contrast, the Civil War is still a hot political topic in America. In part, this may be because it is the only war we have fought among ourselves; though this could be a reason for repressing discussion rather than causing it. For immediate political benefit important aspects of the Civil War are sometimes exaggerated or misinterpreted. This hampers rather than helps in eliminating the residue of the War in our politics, economy and society.

This is particularly true of three aspects of the conflict: its causes; the situation in the North at the time of the war; and the attitudes of the North's leader, Abraham Lincoln. Each is distorted because it is politically significant today. The first has to do with America's current concern with racism; the second has to do with the legitimacy of our nation's political elite; the third has to do with our current president's embracing of Lincoln as his political ideal.

With respect to the origins of the war: power has its reasons to support conflict; wealth has its reasons; and the masses have their reasons. In a democracy, where numbers rule, power and wealth must appeal to the masses for support to go to war in terms the masses accept. Hence, the primary, if not sole, cause generally attributed by the North's leaders to the war as it dragged was to accomplish the abolition of slavery. Economic and partisan political motives were minimized or ignored.

With respect to the situation in the North at the time of the war, there was almost as much exploitation of people in the North, without slavery, as in the South with slavery. In the North exploitation was not of the African-American race, but of the working class.

Southern apologists for slavery pointed to the exploitation of workers practiced by Northern industrialists. In fact, in the same time period of the agitation over slavery, so bad did exploitation of the workforce by industrialists become—and it continued for decades ahead—that there emerged that political horror which was for two centuries to cause countless deaths—Marxist communism. It was in this period that Marx and Engels issued the Communist Manifesto.

But the Southerners, to their discredit, were not proposing to attempt to improve the conditions of the industrial working class in the North (that would only occur more than a half century later). Southerners were instead simply citing one evil (industrial exploitation) to try to justify another (slavery)—which, of course, morally was not legitimate.

Further, Northern industrialists were pleased to seize the anti-slavery agitation as a diversion for the public from their own exploitation of their workforces. Northern industrialists even joked to their slave-owning rivals in the South that slavery had to be abolished because slave-owners were treating their workforces so much better than were Northern industrialists.

Northern industrialists and their descendants who preen themselves on their opposition to slavery were simultaneously availing themselves of the profits of another great evil of human exploitation—that of the working class in factories.

With respect to Lincoln, instead of relating the true motives and deliberations of the President, current apologists offer a smooth surface of events highly varnished to idolize Lincoln as a current political hero. This is particularly true with respect to Lincoln's views of African-Americans which largely reflected the time in which Lincoln lived. Less importantly, current apologists ignore Lincoln's view that Southerners were still American citizens, despite the war.

Lincoln knew that few Southerners were slave holders; that most were fighting not for slavery but for their homeland. At that time many Americans of North and South thought of themselves as from states, first, then from the United States. The Civil War changed that. The states emerged from the War very much reduced in importance. There could no longer be any doubt that a person's first responsibility was to the nation, not to his or her state.

The War Changed the Constitution but Today Both Liberals and Conservatives Deny its Full Significance

Today both liberals and conservatives deny or ignore that the original United States ended in 1861 and emerged in a different form from the Civil War. Many liberals deny this by insisting that the nation was never actually dissolved. The whole legal justification for the Northern war effort was that the South had no legal right to leave the union. Since the North won the war, it also won the legal point that the union was never dissolved.

Liberals also maintain that the current union is based upon consent of all of its people, not just the dominance of a numerical majority or a dominant section. Liberals maintain there was reconciliation after the war; that the South is in the union today voluntarily. They stress that all sections and people are treated alike under American law and that all participate in the same way in the nation's political processes. A majority rules, and it is said to be a majority drawn from all sections of the nation. These positions are necessary to the liberals' political posture as champions of the masses wherever they live; and because it is difficult for liberals to admit that a sizeable minority of the nation are fellow citizens only because of military compulsion—that they are in the United States because they were compelled by war to be. Finally, since there is a pronounced strain of pacifism in today's liberalism, many wish to deny that warfare waged by their predecessors is what held the nation together. Many liberals hold to the proposition that war never settles anything. But, of course, it does. The Civil War settled that the Southern states would remain in the Union and that there would no longer be slavery in the United States.

Many conservatives, for their part, deny the Civil War changed the Constitution by pretending that the original compact—the Constitution of 1789—is still intact, except for the few amendments to the Constitution which quickly followed the Civil War. Conservatives keep seeking to return to the original meaning of the Constitution and the intent of the founders of 1787 as if the dissolution of the original compact and the Civil War and Reconstruction had never occurred. In other words, the Southerners had a view of the meaning of the original Constitution in which federal powers were limited and constrained; a war was fought about the issue and the South lost. The victorious North modified the Constitution to fit its own needs during the war and interpreted it as it preferred, even before amendments were added. Conservatives today hark back to an interpretation of the Constitution similar to that of the South before the Civil War, much as if the war had never happened.

Interpretations of the War Remain a Contest of Moral Impera-tives—Differing Moral Imperatives

The Civil War was so bloody and it involved a moral issue so profound that the American psyche has been riveted to morality in warfare ever since. The roots of the Civil War were economic and political as well as moral. That is, the war was about other things as well as about the moral imperative of ending slavery. But most of us are inclined to evaluate the War solely on a moral basis. Despite our predilection for moral judgments, we have not yet understood simply and directly the basic moral conflict of the Civil War. It was not simply a matter of good versus bad; nor even a matter of the immorality of slavery.

The Civil War was a contest between two different moral imperatives. It was not simply a contest of good against evil. Instead, there was good and evil, right and wrong, on both sides of the Civil War.

The position of the North was that the end (the ending of slavery) justified the means (a war of subjugation and a disavowal of Constitutional protections to wage it). The position of the South was that the means (self-defense, respect of constitutional protections) justified the end (protection of slavery).

Southerners fought to defend the land they lived on. According to Winston Churchill this is the most fundamental right possessed by a human being—to defend his or her home from an invader. It doesn't matter, Churchill added, that the invader may claim the land to be his own (as did the North in the Civil War). That is, in fact, the very problem—that the outsider claims the land for himself and comes with weapons to take possession of it. Southerners, including the large majority who owned no slaves, fought to protect the land on which they lived from outsiders. That was their perspective.

The wrong on the South's side was slavery.

The wrong on the North's side was a war of subjugation and a disavowal of Constitutional requirements in order to wage it. In both instances the bad was so reprehensible that it required justification.

The South defended an immoral institution—slavery—but it fought to protect its homeland. Many Southerners were noble, courageous and sacrificing in protecting their homes, while also in pursuit of a bad cause. The North fought for a moral result—the abolition of slavery—but it employed highly questionable means. It invaded other people's land; it waged war on civilians; it disregarded its own Constitution in its actions; it released the rich from military service while it conscripted the poor, and slaughtered people protesting conscription.

We are very familiar with the principle of the end justifying the means; and generally we reject it on moral grounds. But it isn't rejected when most of us consider its application by the North during the Civil War. Instead, we justify all actions taken by the North in the war on the grounds that they contributed to an end of slavery.

Most of us don't think about the principle that the means justify the end very much; yet we rely on it greatly. In fact, our criminal justice system is based on little else. We don't generally know if a defendant is guilty or not; we know that a jury has convicted or acquitted the defendant. If the jury has convicted him, we presume he is guilty and imprison or execute him. If the jury has acquitted him, we ignore later evidence that he is guilty, saying that we in America reject double jeopardy (a second trial based on new evidence). So in either situation, it is the means—the procedure of a jury trial—that justifies the end, the punishment or release of the defendant.

Although we rely in court on the means, a jury trial, to justify the end, the verdict, we know that it is an imperfect system, that a jury is sometimes wrong in its verdict. This is one of the key arguments against the death penalty, that a person convicted by a jury may well be innocent and we should not risk executing people who might someday be found to have been innocent.

We rely on the principle that the means justifies the end in our civil law as well. Suppose a father dies and in his will leaves his entire estate to his son and nothing to three daughters. The result doesn't seem to us fair; but if the legal forms are all properly done, then the result is legally acceptable. The means has justified the end.

One of the most striking aspects of the American Civil War, and rarely commented upon by historians, is the enormous human price paid by the South in its effort to achieve independence. Of the Southern white male population able to bear arms, some 39 percent died in the war. The seriously wounded and crippled from the war constituted an unknown additional reduction in Southern manpower.

A comparable figure for dead among North manpower (which includes slaves who resided in the South, more than 100,000 of whom served in the Union army during the war) was nine percent. The proportionate death toll of Southern white males is among the largest in the history of warfare. In fact, the South simply ran out of manpower to fill its armies, and collapsed militarily in consequence. In general, this was a war in which a very large proportion of the combatant population died fighting against an overwhelmingly superior opponent.

For Southerners, the Civil War was fought courageously, even nobly, and so it acquires a justification which otherwise it would not have. Preserving slavery was an ignoble objective, and so the end cannot be justified directly. But the courage and sacrifice of Southerners in fighting the War was its own justification for the War, just as a jury trial is its own justification for the outcome of the trial.

Motivations for the Masses

The motives for war are usually those of the elite—motives of economic enrichment and political empowerment. This was the case in the Civil War. But the elite do not fight wars; the masses do. This was very true of the Civil War in which the Union permitted men who had the resources to do so to pay substitutes to fight for them.

It was, the poor complained, "a rich man's war and a poor man's fight." This slogan was the rallying cry of rioters in New York City in 1863 protesting conscription into the Union army. During the riots some 2,000 protesters are said to have been killed by police and Union troops.

Because Southerners fought to save their homes from invaders, the South never needed a popular cause to motivate its defenders. It had one.

Lincoln, recognizing that the North had no such widely popular and moral basis to motivate its people, found a popular moral cause (a cause for which people were prepared to die or see their loved ones die) in the abolition of slavery. Lincoln acted outside the Constitution in issuing the Emancipation Proclamation and justified it as a necessary act of war in defense of the Union. He argued that the elimination of slavery would deprive the South of necessary support for its war production. Because at the time that the Emancipation Proclamation was issued, the Proclamation applied only to areas not in control of Union forces—that is, it applied only where it could not be implemented—this was a thin rationale. In reality, the Proclamation was intended to stir war fervor in the North, and this it did successfully. In this respect, Lincoln was correct in describing the Proclamation as a necessary aspect of the Northern war effort.

The Causes of the War

There are two positions about the causes of the American Civil War. One holds that the war was first and foremost about slavery. The other holds that the war was rooted in economic differences between the sections of the nation that went much deeper than slavery. According to the second position, slavery alone would not have provoked the war.

If, as so many people insist, the Civil War was primarily about ending slavery, then it was one of the most unusual conflicts in history. A war of four years duration was fought by the North at the price of hundreds of thousands dead and more hundreds of thousands wounded. It was fought, according to this commonly accepted point of view, in order to bring freedom to people of different geography and a different race. The war was not begun nor fought nor won by the slaves themselves, though some 100,000 former slaves fought in the Union army and several thousand died. The war was the effort of people of one race on behalf of the freedom of people of a different race whom they didn't know personally. It is very hard, if not impossible, to find a parallel in history of such disinterested generosity by one race or nation on behalf of another.

It may be argued that Northerners had ulterior motives of an economic, political or even social nature. This may be true, but then the war wasn't really about slavery at all, and slavery was only a pretense for the ulterior motives. It was one or the other—a war about slavery and a remarkable effort of altruism, or a war not about slavery and a much more conventional motivation.

Possibly the war wasn't primarily about abolishing slavery. In fact, Abraham Lincoln repeatedly and consistently denied that the war was about slavery. The war was, Lincoln insisted, to preserve the Union and not to limit or abolish slavery. His issuance of the Emancipation Proclamation, Lincoln always explained, was merely a war measure intended to weaken the Southern states in their war-making capacity.

In order to affirm that they were right in their use of deadly force against their fellow citizens, people of the victorious North resort, even today, to certain pretensions. They assert that the war was primarily for the purpose of abolishing slavery, and that all Americans now recognize that slavery should have been abolished. Thus the war was nothing more than a disagreement about slavery, and it turned out that the North was both right and victorious and that was the end of the matter—an unfortunate experience which is now fully behind us.

Was the War about slavery or not? The answer is that it was and it wasn't primarily about slavery. For the Northern and Southern elites the War was always about economics and political power. For the abolitionists of the North it was always about slavery. For the masses of the North in the beginning it was about patriotism. But over time and as the casualties mounted, the Northern masses were excited to a fever pitch by anti-slavery rhetoric. For the firebrands of the South the War was always about slavery. For the masses of the South it was always about protecting their homes from invasion.

The result of war is usually determined by the passions of those who fight it—the masses. This Lincoln realized. In order to arouse the passions of the masses, he issued the Emancipation Proclamation. The Proclamation aroused passions on each side of the conflict. Those passions roil our politics yet.

PART TWO

Our Lingering Heritage is a Joint Responsibility of North and South

CHAPTER FIVE

Slavery Was Ended But Not Sufficiently Remedied

The history of emancipation of African-Americans from slavery and segregation in America is one of great political advance but insufficient economic progress. At the time of the Civil War slaves were freed and given political rights, but economic progress eluded them. This is still the pattern today. It is a lingering heritage of slavery which underlies today's persisting racism.

Strong Political but Weak Economic Advance

In general, the African-American community in the United States has made substantial political progress since the onset of the Civil War, but far less relative economic progress. Instead of dealing effectively with the economic challenge and its various causes, the North and South have preferred to argue over the moral interpretation of the War.

These are lingering shadows of the War: economic deprivation in the African-American community; disregard in the white community of deprivation in the African-American community except when it can be made an occasion for political gain.

In the course of American history, African-American people have repeatedly received political rights but not economic progress. Instead, today African-American people largely remain de facto segregated residentially, especially in the North. African-Americans live where the jobs are not. Residential segregation serves the political advantage of their political champions, but residential segregation provides no significant material advantage to African-Americans. Originally the political champions of African-Americans who benefitted from residential segregation were Republicans; now they're Democrats.

Martin Luther King's March on Washington in 1963, for example, was formally "a march for jobs and freedom." The result was an extension of political freedom (in particular, the Voting Rights Act) but few jobs if any. The March achieved much in the area of freedom; it achieved little in the area of jobs. This is the story of the African-American community in America since emancipation; it is as much the responsibility of the North as of the South.

The most glaring example is the most recent. With the election of an African-American president of the United States, the political success of African-Americans generally had reached a new, high point. But in the years of his presidency, the economic difficulties of African-Americans generally reached a level not known since the end of the Great Depression.

Meanwhile, the political careers of tens of thousands of office holders in America, mostly white—primarily Republicans until the Great Depression, and primarily Democrats since —have been advanced and their personal fortunes enhanced (since the government of the American Republic has from the Civil War been largely corrupt) via African-American voting support.

Ever since it won the Civil War the North has had the capacity to improve the economic lot of the African-American community far more than has been done. In fact, since African-American people are now widely distributed throughout the United States, something that has occurred since the Civil War, the North could have done much for African-American people in its own geographic area. At the time of emancipation most African-American people lived in the South so that whatever was to be done for them had to be accomplished in the South. This was difficult. Union armies were followed by large numbers of freed slaves without means of economic support. A common slogan of the time was "Forty acres and a mule." The notion was that freed slaves would receive a homestead to farm. For a variety of reasons, this initiative failed. Instead, former slaves often went back to work for their former masters, not as slaves but as sharecroppers, and lived in the same poverty as when they were slaves. They had the right to vote, and to leave their farms, but that is all that had changed for them. They had nowhere to go and no support for going there.

The war was followed by indifference to the fate of freed slaves; massive political corruption and exploitation of the weak. Napoleon once commented, "When I spoke to the Polish serfs (slaves) about liberty, they answered, 'Certainly, we should like to have it very much, but who will feed, clothe and house us?" Freed slaves in America had the same concern. The victorious federal government failed almost totally in its responsibility to ameliorate the economic plight of slaves who were freed. For many decades freed slaves and their children and grandchildren lived in abject poverty.

In the immediate aftermath of the Civil War, the North failed to educate and empower the slaves economically. It empowered them politically for Northern purposes outside the South; then it abandoned them to Jim Crow in the South. Decades later it supported the efforts of the Civil Rights Movement to end Jim Crow. But these political initiatives were not accompanied by effective economic initiatives. (We might note that something very similar occurred in South Africa after the end of apartheid provided political rights to black South Africans.)

It is interesting to speculate why. At one level the white Northern electorate was not prepared to tolerate political exploitation of African-American people in the South, but it was prepared to tolerate economic exploitation of African-American people all over the country. At a deeper level, the political powers of the moment in the North saw themselves able to benefit from the political liberation of African-American people in the South, but not from their economic advance.

Sharecropping was usually a miserable livelihood and as opportunities arose African-Americans migrated north. Sometimes they went to job opportunities in the factories of the North; sometimes to jobs in service industries. Over time, African-Americans spread over the country, with only New England, the center of the abolitionist effort before and during the Civil War, and the upper plains states continuing to have few African-American residents. The low level of racial mixture in New England is viewed as ironic in the North and as hypocritical in the South.

In the 1930s and again in the 1960s when African-Americans came north, the North refused to integrate them. That was the origin of today's ghettos and the subculture of young male violence and imprisonment. It is a subculture of fatherless families, built in large part on de facto segregation and lack of economic opportunity.

African-Americans who left the South went overwhelmingly to ghettos in the big cities of the Mid-Atlantic, Midwestern and Pacific states. Some who got good jobs in factories during World War II lost them in the hollowing out of the national economy in the years after 1980. Most manufacturing jobs were either outsourced abroad or downgraded in pay and benefits—a process driven by the financial services industry which is headquartered in the Northeast. It was the Northeast which deprived the African-American community (along with whites) of the middle class jobs they had found in manufacturing. This process was a continuation of that which originated in the Civil War by which the North provided political but not economic gains to African-Americans.

The North prefers to ignore this record. The South had no direct hand in the failure to integrate African-American people into the full economic life of the North, but neither did it object or do better itself.

Why Have the Economic Fortunes of the African-American Community Been Limited?

Several explanations are offered. There is the failure of the American white community to fully integrate African-American people into the social (in particular the residential) and economic life of the nation. There is continued residential segregation of our cities. In essence, African-American job seekers are not located where the jobs are located.

Another level of explanation involves limitations in the African-American community generally which contribute to lack of general economic success. For example, there is the relatively low level of education in the African-American community. But why is the education level in the African-American community relatively weak? Part of the explanation involves a lack of investment in education for the African-American community by the larger society. Another part of the explanation involves a lack of commitment to education by the African-American community, including a general acceptance in the African-American community of the American popular culture with its lack of emphasis on education.

Not all lessons learned in the anti-slavery struggle are still accepted. One of the worst aspects of slavery was that many slaveholders tried to keep slaves from being educated; in particular from learning to read. Early African-American leaders understood this and championed education for former slaves. They saw that education was very valuable. Yet this aggressive attitude toward education has almost disappeared from African-American community. Today Bill Cosby and supporters are trying to revive a positive attitude toward higher education via TV ads and other means.

Some observers point to the destruction of the family unit as a key factor in limiting African-American economic success. Slavery didn't respect the nuclear family, and the pattern set then has become common in the African-American community. Some 80 percent of African-American children today are reported to be in single parent families.

CHAPTER SIX

Political Echos from the War

The strong emotionalism of American politics and our preference for inexperienced national leaders are important aspects of American politics today. Each is an echo from the Civil War.

Emotionalism Trumps Reason

It has been noted by historians that the South need not have left the Union; it did so in a fit of anger upon the election of Abraham Lincoln. The South was well-protected politically in the Congress. That slavery would not be spreading to the new states which were entering the Union had already been essentially determined. But there was little likelihood that slavery in the states where it existed would be in danger. The South had sufficient protection for slavery within the Congress and under the Constitution over a number of coming years. The genius of the American Constitution lay in majority rule with checks and balances. The South in the mid-19th century was falling into a perpetual minority, but it had protection in Constitutional checks and balances. Further, the Supreme Court had ruled in favor of Northern states having to recognize the rights of people to property in slaves. On balance, there seems to have been no immediate crisis for the South raised by the election of Lincoln.

But Southern hotheads had so agitated the public mind in the states of the Deep South that what appears to have been merely anger at Lincoln's election led directly to the secession of several states from the Union. The election of Lincoln—representing a new Party, the Republicans, who had first contested a presidential election only four years before and which was closely associated with the abolitionists —was interpreted by many Southerners as a provocation. The response of the South to provocation was to try to leave the Union.

When the South left the Union, it permitted the North to exert majority rule without checks and balances. The form of the checks and balances remained, but the reality had changed dramatically. So the South had done great damage to itself by leaving the Union. It had lost its Constitutional protections. In retrospect, it appears that it was not a reasoned concern for the future of slavery and the cotton-based economy of the Deep South that led to secession, but rather sheer emotionalism.

During the war the emotionalism of the South was maintained by a moral fervor based on the North's invasion of the South. Southerners were called upon by their leaders to expel the invaders. The moral principle involved was the sanctity of hearth and home.

Thus, in the South throughout the war emotional commitment was kept alive by moral indignation.

According to Northern historians, particularly Bruce Catton, the North also employed moral indignation to maintain an emotional attachment to its cause. This was necessary because emotionalism and moralism are not the same, but are related. Moral outrage or moral commitment, or both, can be used to create and maintain a high level of emotionalism or enthusiasm.

This is not a matter of moral argument. Moral argument is needed for elites, especially in the Anglo-Saxon world. This is a matter of moral emotionalism—of indignation and anger rooted in moral outrage which spurs the masses to commitment.

Many people in the Anglo-Saxon world project their concerns about morality in politics onto other societies. They believe that there is a court of public opinion that transcends national and cultural boundaries to which all parties to a conflict must appeal. Thus, every side to a conflict strives to occupy the moral "high ground." Failure to do so is a likely cause of defeat. So powerful is public opinion, the argument goes, that wars involving terror cannot be waged—a topic to which we will return later in this book.

Possibly, the opposite is the case. Instead of the moral authority of public opinion growing in the world, it may well be declining, especially in its home ground of the Anglo-Saxon world. Ours is an age of decaying moral concern—one in which a media spokesperson for the Administration can describe belief in personal moral standards as evidence of cultural backwardness—it may be difficult to believe that moral outrage can motivate emotional commitment to a military struggle. But this is what happened in the American Civil War.

The problem which Lincoln faced was not one of the commitment of Union soldiers, but of the civilian population—of the electorate—in the North. As it became evident that the war was going to be long and bloody, there was a danger that the Northern electorate would cease to support the war and the sacrifices necessary to win it.

The early enthusiasm in the North for war to preserve the Union seemed after a year of costly battles to be ebbing. A new source of emotional commitment was needed for the electorate of the North. Lincoln determined to provide it by taking steps toward the abolition of slavery.

Before and during the War, leaders on both sides used emotions to stir up the populace. We have done so often since the Civil War. Our leaders have often hidden their real purposes for going to war, pointing instead to atrocities (World War I), sneak attacks (the Spanish-American War and World War II), etc. These causes for war are intended to stir popular emotions.

The American entrance to the First World War is a most interesting case of emotionalism driving America into war, because America should probably have stayed out of the war. The American entry was decisive in giving victory to the Allies. But out of victory emerged a whole set of disasters. Had America not entered World War I, then the war might well have ended in a stalemate with a peace agreement in 1917; neither side would have won the war. Had there been peace in 1917 instead of at the end of 1918, and had there been no defeat of Germany and no Versailles Treaty, then there would have been no Russian Communist Revolution, no rise of Fascism in Italy and Spain, no Nazi Germany, no World War II and no Cold War.

Americans have trouble accepting reasons of international politics as justification for war (as in Korea, Vietnam, Iraq or Afghanistan) or not for war (as in World War I), and so we disguise such motives in two ways—one with emotion, the other with morality; and, of course, the two are linked. People get emotional about what they perceive to be moral questions. And for most people emotions—love, hate, outrage, pity, fear, and resentment —drive opinions and actions.

There has for centuries been a tendency in the Anglo-Saxon world to moralize about actions. This is why so much of the rest of the world, including the French who articulate the matter most clearly, see us as more hypocritical than most other societies. In this perspective, the experience of the Civil War was simply an extension of an Anglo-Saxon propensity; yet in the Civil War that propensity was repeated and extended. Lincoln introduced into the war an emotional and moral aspect which sustained the North to victory.

The people of the United States are able, one might say willing, to sustain to victory only short conflicts unless they have a strong emotional/moral motivation. A few subsequent American presidents, who have not profited from Lincoln's example, have failed to win the conflicts they have conducted. The best example is the Vietnam War—a long, bloody conflict for which Lyndon Johnson never found a persuasive moral motivation. The result was disaster—public support for the war collapsed. A similar process occurred in the Iraqi and Afghan wars—an extended argument about American self-defense was inadequate to sustain long conflicts without a moral motivation. The initial emotion created by the attack on the World Trade Center weakened with time and with no substantial moral motivation to sustain war support, the conflicts had to be abandoned. Protection of the rights of women and girls from fundamentalist Islamic prejudice was offered by feminist groups and by Presidents Bush and Obama as a moral justification for the Iraqi and Afghan wars. But a moral crusade for this purpose failed to be widely adopted by the American electorate.

In general, the United States, from the Civil War onward, has been especially subject to emotional and moral motivations for war. Generally, American politicians and our electorate cannot stand the moral ambiguity of war motivated by national interests and international politics. So we either pick sides (like Senator John McCain has done in the Syrian conflict) or we seek refuge in a moral posture (as Barack Obama has done). Military efforts for reasons of international politics occur in America in an environment of public opinion that makes it difficult to gain support for them.

In general, we may say that the causes of war are elite (economic) and popular (emotional). When recourse can be had successfully by political leaders to emotion, then the psychology of the masses is largely indifferent to reality. As is so readily apparent from the Civil War, in politics, emotionalism often triumphs.

As abolitionists in the North ever-more vigorously opposed slavery, Southern radicals in response supported slavery ever more strongly. Radicals on each side engaged radicals on the other side and both exerted influence far beyond their numbers.

Objective Southerners saw that the South could not win a war with the North and tried to avoid it. Sam Houston, the winner of Texas's independence from Mexico, destroyed his political career opposing secession.

"I tell you..." Houston told a crowd in Galveston, "the North is determined to preserve this union. They are not a fiery and impulsive people as you are...But when they begin to move in a given direction...they move with the steady momentum and perseverance of a mighty avalanche, and... they will overwhelm the South in ignoble defeat."

Despite Houston's all too accurate warning, Texas seceded from the Union and was ultimately overwhelmed in defeat.

In fiction, Rhett Butler, hero of *Gone With the Wind*, opposed secession from the standpoint of reason—"the North is too strong for us"—only to be shouted down by the belligerent firebrands of the South.

Some Southerners hoped for a future of expansion and profit in which the South, freed of Northern commercial exploitation, would build an empire in the Caribbean and Central America. Southern adventurers, "filibusters" in the terminology of the time, had already invaded Central America seeking to create political units that could later be attached to an independent South. Finally, many Southerners were incensed at continual Northern interference in what the Southerners considered to be their internal affairs.

The elites excited the masses using various themes. This is usually a pattern—the elites excite the masses for the hidden purposes of the elites. One sees this pattern everywhere. For example, today elites in the Muslim world care little or nothing about Palestine, but it is the issue used to excite the masses and to divert their attention from issues within the Muslim world which are threatening to the elites. At the time of the American Civil War the Northern elite who were exploiting workers in the factories used slavery to excite the emotions of the masses against an economic rival in the South and in order to distract attention of the workers from exploitation.

Southern elites, leaving the poor whites of the South to suffer in poverty and ignorance, used the prospect of Northern invasion to excite the emotions of the masses against an economic rival in the North and in order to distract attention from the deprivation and political impotence of the poor at home in the South.

The Civil War was generated by the elites in their economic conflict with each other, but it was fought, and therefore many considered caused, by the masses in the North about slavery and in the South about the Northern invasion. Economics was the remote cause; slavery was a proximate cause.

Secession was whipped on by emotion. It was clear to all thinking people that the South would be very hard-pressed to defeat the North in a military conflict. But Southern zealots insisted that Southern courage would prevail over Northern weaponry and numbers. This is an emotional argument often made in favor of war: "One of our people can defeat several of theirs; the enemy lacks the courage to fight." Many Southerners seem to have bought the argument at the outset of the War.

Emotionalism causes people to do things that reason would have had them avoid. For example, when people are highly emotional, warning them of danger doesn't cause them to avoid it. The South left the Union, as we have seen, in a fit of anger. Secession was a terribly mistaken decision which reason would have rejected.

When emotion is in charge, it's folly to expect people to do what it is in their own best interests to do. The Civil War has left America with a legacy of emotionalism in politics. As a result, America is unable to lead wisely. It can lead morally, but not wisely. In consequence, many of its interventions on moral bases (such as human rights, democracy, anti-weapons of mass destruction) make things even worse. This is a result of Americans' addiction to a romantic morality in politics rather than to realism, as if every conflict needs to be made a war to free the slaves. This is a significant aspect of the continuing shadows of our Civil War.

Choosing Inexperienced Leaders and Paying a Price

Lincoln had great qualities and is deservedly revered by the nation. His success in the Civil War both preserved the Union and freed the slaves. There is suggestive evidence that had he survived the war, he might have led a more effective integration of former slaves into American society and reintegration of the Southern states into the Union. It was a tragedy for all that he was assassinated.

When Lincoln was elected president, he had little experience of national politics. He knew the key issues, but not the levers of national power. He knew few of the Southern leaders. Had Lincoln had more experience of politics—meaning the personalities, attitudes and processes involved—at the national level, the war might have been avoided.

Once in the war, Lincoln was able to win it, and this is a very important thing. It's what history remembers and celebrates. Lincoln's position in the pantheon of American heroes is strong evidence for the proposition that what matters in a leader's record is that he or she got the big things right. Lincoln preserved the Union and ended slavery. These were the big things. The costs are now ignored, as are any less costly alternatives that might have existed at the time. But the nation would have been better off, then and now, without the enormous costs incurred by Lincoln's approach to preserving the Union and ending slavery. Avoiding war would have been better for the nation in that it would have preserved many lives and saved the South from economic ruin.

We could take a different attitude toward the War. We could say that it was an unqualified good; that in this instance war was better than any alternative. If we take the position that the nation was better served by having the war than not by having it, then we are giving war an unqualified endorsement in the circumstances of 1861. We are saying that war was better than non-war for America.

It is likely that most Americans would be reluctant to endorse the War if war could have been avoided without sacrificing the Union and the end of slavery. In considering Lincoln's poor preparation for the presidency, we are forcing ourselves to confront a common contradiction in American opinion: that it is better to resolve matters without war so that to have avoided the Civil War was better than to have fought it; and on the other hand that by the Civil War Lincoln accomplished important objectives and so justified war, at least in this instance.

This contradiction endures in the American psyche. In 2014 our nation wishes to avoid involvement in war in the Middle East, but wishes to accomplish objectives which likely cannot be achieved without war—including regime change in Syria and the exclusion of chemical and nuclear weapons from use in the region.

If we admit that the United States might have been better served by avoiding civil war in 1861, then we must also admit that choosing for president a man as little experienced as Lincoln was costly to the nation. We must also admit that, in general, electing poorly experienced presidents involves risks to the nation. We have done this three times beginning in 1992 and the nation has suffered a series of unfortunate wars. The last American war that has had a salutary effect was that waged by President George H. W. Bush to free Kuwait from Iraqi conquest. President George H. W. Bush was well-prepared for his position by service in the federal government. His successors have not been.

The Civil War, like all other wars, was a contest. It was a race to victory between two contestants—North and South. In any race there are two ways to win: by outrunning the other contestant or by finishing when the other contestant trips and falls. When a contestant wins the second way, it wasn't because he was faster or better trained, it was because he benefitted from the misfortune or error of his opponent.

Lincoln's victory in the Civil War was as much or more due to the limitations and failures of his opponents as to his own qualities. It is fair, therefore, to look with a critical eye at him as a leader.

Had Lincoln had more political experience at the national level (he had a limited amount of experience from serving as a one-term Congressman more than a decade before he was elected President), the war might have been avoided.

Had Lincoln had more military experience (he had virtually none), the war might have been greatly shortened and much suffering avoided for all involved: civilians, soldiers and slaves. This is because Lincoln was not a good selector of generals most of the time, and because he insisted on micro-managing the war much of the time.

The one chance to avert war after a Republican was elected president was to persuade Virginia to stay in the Union. Without Virginia the Confederacy was not economically or militarily viable. Instead of the course it took, the South might have stayed in the

Union with either of two objectives. It might have sought to protect slavery using Constitutional checks and balances in its favor. Conversely, the South might have agreed to a process for extinguishing slavery. This was, of course, the option that was best for the long-term benefit of the South. Lincoln was offering ideas for such a process, and many of the South's leaders, including those like Robert E. Lee who would command its armies against the North, were in favor of an end to slavery. Senator Stephen A. Douglas of Illinois tried to persuade Northerners to reject Lincoln on the grounds that he was a provocation to the South, and to choose himself, Douglas, the presidential offering of the Democratic Party, as a candidate who could avoid conflict. So there was a peace candidate, but the North chose Lincoln instead.

Confronted with the secession of the Deep South, President Lincoln did not know how to get Virginia to stay in the Union. The result was our Civil War.

Lincoln has been judged a great politician. The judgment reflects his effectiveness in holding divisive tendencies in the North together sufficiently to win the war. Such a favorable judgment of Lincoln is reached by ignoring his failure to meet the challenge of avoiding war altogether.

Warfare might have been avoided had Lincoln possessed the political skills to do so. The challenge was great—hotheads in North and South wanted war. Southern firebrands were demanding secession. Still, Lincoln had been elected president of the entire country. Had he had the experience and skills to bring about an accommodation, war might not have occurred. Andrew Jackson had faced a similar crisis when he was in office and avoided both secession and war.

When Lincoln took office in 1861 there were many possible grounds upon which an accommodation to avoid war might have been based. Lincoln ended up a war president because he couldn't avoid the war. He almost lost the War—but Lee's overreach at Gettysburg gave Lincoln victory. Lincoln lost the opportunity for peace but won the War. He is remembered as a great president because he won the War, and is forgiven his failure to avoid it.

The assertion here is that had a president been selected in 1860 who possessed more experience in the national political scene than Lincoln, the Civil War in the particularly virulent form it took might have been avoided. The strongest argument for this assertion is that avoiding war was so much in the interest of the South, which after all, was fated to lose it. Nevertheless, that war might have been avoided is necessarily a conjecture. It cannot be demonstrated that a different outcome would have resulted had another president than Lincoln been elected. But it's hard to believe that a more experienced president-elect could have done worse in terms of starting the war. Warfare was not avoided; enough states seceded to form a viable political entity (a nation) including creating from scratch an army able to sustain a four-year war; the North lost the major initial battles; the President's choices for military commanders were often so poor that the war was prolonged. A President-elect who was more experienced in national politics and in military matters might have avoided war or minimized it.

Americans have a penchant for electing relatively inexperienced presidents, and both the United States and the world pay a price—sometimes a very high one. For example, during his presidential terms Theodore Roosevelt played a major role as peace-maker in the world. He brought the contestants in the Russo-Japanese War to the negotiating table and to peace. Several times he intervened in European great power disputes to avoid a major war in Europe. In 1912 the United States electorate rejected TR's bid for reelection. Instead, our people elected Woodrow Wilson. Wilson was an intelligent, idealistic man with experience as a college president (Princeton) and a governor (New Jersey). What he didn't know about European great power politics was a lot.

When war suddenly loomed on the European horizon in the summer of 1914, Wilson was unable to avert it. World War I began. It is possible that TR might have been successful in avoiding the war. Once the war was underway, TR supported the Allies (Britain, France and Russia) strongly. However, TR had the experience to possibly have avoided the war; Wilson did not. The world might have saved millions of lives and avoided World War II (which grew directly out of World War I), had TR been in a position to try avert the onset of war.

A common confusion arises here. People who respect the military are often presumed to be militarists—that is, people who seek war. The opposite is often the case. Generals in high office often avoid war. TR had been a colonel, never a general, but he had avoided war during his presidency (as did George Washington, U. S. Grant and Dwight Eisenhower, for example) and instead had used the American military which he had supported strengthening (only Congress can appropriate the money to do so) to help bring peace to troubled areas of the globe. He might have been able to do so to avoid the First World War.

More is involved than experience. Sometimes presidents are sufficiently experienced but are not effective enough leaders. For example, Franklin Delano Roosevelt was experienced in international affairs when he was elected president. He recognized almost immediately the danger Hitler's Germany presented to world peace. So during the 1930s Roosevelt struggled to get the American public to support action against Hitler while Germany was still weak. He was right to do so. But he couldn't persuade the people or the Congress to take action in time. Perhaps a more skillful leader could have done so. This is despite the fact that FDR is generally considered a very skillful politician.

Confederate President Jefferson Davis was a far more experienced military person than Lincoln. He had the ability to persuade Robert E. Lee to head Confederate forces in Virginia and to leave him largely alone to do so except for such support as Davis could provide. The war was not won for the South by Davis's ability to choose a key commander, but it was much lengthened.

Lincoln, in contrast, experimented for almost three years of war before identifying the team of generals who were able to win it. FDR, again in contrast to Lincoln, had considerable naval experience before World War II and quickly hit upon the combination of top officers who would win the war for America.

Perhaps a more skilled politician than Lincoln might have been able to avoid war or to win it more quickly and efficiently. Key capabilities a different president would have had to possess are deep acquaintance with the major national political figures of the time and enough military knowledge to obtain excellent military commanders for the Union and allow them to prosecute the war.

PART THREE

The Sections Remain

CHAPTER SEVEN

A Sectional Fault Line Defined in the Civil War Is the Most Important Factor in American Presidential Politics

Today's Presidential elections begin with a Southern base of reliable states for the Republicans and a Northeastern and Far Western base of reliable states for the Democrats. This sectional division is a direct result of the Civil War. Elections are decided, therefore, by "swing" states—those not already committed to one party of the other. Today there are only some ten states that swing elections for the other 40.

The Sectional Boundary in Presidential Politics

The boundary between Northeast and South remains the major fault line in American politics. A person who watches the great sectional division of America will never go far wrong in understanding current events and in predicting future directions in American politics.

The division of the United States which occurred at the time of the Civil War into politically antagonistic sections remains to this day. It is generally and intentionally ignored in our political discussions and controversies. But under the surface the deep division sometimes emerges into public view. It is always there. It is the major legacy of the War and has its origins before the American Revolution.

In its most fundamental aspect, the politics of the United States involves the rivalry of Northeast and South and their respective attempts to attract the political support of the West and Midwest. For example, it is surprising how long Ohio has been the key state in national elections. Maybe that's why so many presidents in the post-Civil War era came from Ohio (Garfield, Hayes, McKinley, Taft, and Harding).

An examination of state by state returns in recent Presidential elections reveals the continuing contest of the Northeast and South for the support of the Midwest. The Northeastern states, the core of the old Union, support Democratic presidential candidates repeatedly. The states of the old Confederacy support Republican presidential candidates repeatedly. Elections are decided by the shifting views of Border, Midwestern and Mountain states. This reflects exactly the sectional division of the nation at the time of the Civil War, though, as we shall see, the complexion of the political parties has changed in the sections.

There are certain exceptions. Florida, which was a state of the Confederacy, but which now contains many people who migrated from the Northeast and upper Midwest, is a swing state—sometimes voting Republican and sometimes Democratic.

The states which at the time of the Civil War were considered Border States have largely chosen sides. Kentucky ordinarily joins the Southern states in a national election; Missouri and Maryland ordinarily join the states of the Union. Virginia, not usually considered a border state, but actually the most important of them all, shifts back and forth as befits a true Border State.

It is possible to attribute the opposition to the Democratic presidential candidate in most Southern states during the past two elections to continuing racism in those states. It was the fact that the Democratic candidate was a person of color; it might be thought that caused the Southern states to vote against him. There is likely some truth in this. But the persistence of Southern support for the Republican candidates in many previous presidential elections, and for the Democratic candidates before that (that is, before the pirouette of the two political parties which is described below), when there was not an African-American candidate running, suggests that there is much more to the story than racism alone.

The Early Political Affiliation of the North and South

The Democratic Party traces its origins to Thomas Jefferson. In the most recent century, the Democrats have pursued a reputation as the party of the people, and as a party that detests racism. Yet Jefferson's Democratic Party introduced party partisanship into the US in the 1790s for the ultimate, and secret, purpose of preserving slavery. George Washington warned the nation in his letter to the American people—referred to as his Farewell Address—to avoid the spirit of faction or partisan politics. But it was already abroad in the land. Jefferson feared that the North, organizing itself as the Federalist Party, would use the power of the new central government to begin to restrict and abolish slavery. Such actions were being threatened at the time by Northern representatives in the Congress. Jefferson's populism was understood in the South as having a hidden agenda of preserving slavery. The South became closely attached to the Democratic Party. (This point, uncomfortable for many Americans today, is convincingly made by J.J. Ellis in *Founding Brothers*, New York: Random House, 2000.)

Jefferson's Democratic Party had from the first a strong foothold in the South and the Border States. But there was nothing solid or unvarying about it. Over the presidential elections which occurred before the Civil War, Southern states sometimes voted for Democratic presidential candidates; sometimes for Whig presidential candidates; and sometimes for National Republican presidential candidates.

The Northeast was the stronghold of the Federalist Party in the early days of the nation. But repeated victories by the Democrats in presidential elections slowly eroded the Federalist Party until after 1816 it disappeared.

In 1856 when the Republican Party first fielded a presidential candidate, most Northeastern states supported him. The Democrats, with primarily Southern support, captured the presidency.

During the Civil War various factions of the Democratic Party supported slavery and opposed the war. In the North most Democrats were opposed to abolition and were prepared to let the Southern states depart from the Union. They campaigned against Lincoln's election in both 1860 and 1864. Yet today, Democrats claim Lincoln as if he were one of their own.

At the time of the Civil War the United States had two sections which dominated its politics—the Northeast which was Republican and the South which was Democratic. The Midwest vacillated between them. This was the political complexion of the Civil War and it dominated American national politics without challenge for the four years of the Civil War and for 65 years after.

The Civil War Cemented the Political Division of the Nation into Two Key Sections

The Civil War grew out of an election that was thoroughly sectional. Abraham Lincoln, the candidate of the Republican Party (which had emerged only a few years before) carried no states outside the Northeast and North Central sections. Lincoln carried not a single Border State. He was elected with only 40 percent of the nation's popular vote. The Deep South, soon to leave the Union, voted Democratic; the Border States, especially Virginia, voted for a third party whose purpose was to avoid the division of the Union and likely war.

From 1860 forward for two decades presidential elections were caught up in the dislocations created by war and reconstruction. The Republicans won each of those elections: 1864, 1868, 1872 and 1876.

The first real post-Civil War presidential election was held in 1880.

In 1880 the Civil War had been over for 15 years, but its impact on American national politics continued.

In 1880 the Republicans won the presidency without taking a Southern or a border state.

In 1884 the Democrats finally won the presidency again—it had been 24 years since they had held the White House. To win the Democrats took the South and Border States and cut into the Republican North by running a governor of New York, Grover Cleveland, for the presidency. New York supported its former governor and combined with the South to win the election for the Democrats.

Four years later the Republicans recaptured the White House in a strictly sectional election. The Republicans won all the Northern states; the Democrats won all the Southern and border states.

In 1892 Grover Cleveland won reelection for the Democrats. The Democrats won the South, Border States and bit into the North with victories in New York and Illinois.

The pattern of American national elections was clear. The North would vote Republican; the South would vote Democratic. Victory would go to the party which could win the Border States or could make inroads into the stronghold of the other party—as the Democrats did both times Grover Cleveland won the presidency when they took New York State from the Republicans.

In 1896 the Republicans again captured the presidency relying on Northeastern and Midwestern votes. The South voted Democrat.

In 1900 McKinley won reelection for the Republicans, but he was soon assassinated and his vice-president, Theodore Roosevelt (TR) took the office of President. In 1900 the South had voted Democrat.

In 1904 Theodore Roosevelt was elected in his own right. The South voted against him; all the rest of the country voted for him. The Republicans captured 70 percent of the electoral vote—much larger than the usual margins in American presidential elections up to that time. The South was solidly Democratic, but isolated politically.

In 1908 William Howard Taft won election for the Republicans. The South and a few western states opposed his election.

In 1912 TR split the Republican vote by challenging Taft for the presidency. The Democrat candidate, Woodrow Wilson, slipped into the office of President with only 42 percent of the popular vote but 82 percent of the electoral vote. Wilson carried the South and most of the country; but most of the popular vote in the Northern states went to one of the two Republican candidates. Theodore Roosevelt had run on the Bull Moose Party ticket, but all understood that he was a Republican in all but label. The sectional pattern asserted itself in popular voting if not in Electoral College results.

In 1916 Woodrow Wilson won reelection in a close contest in which the South and West supported the Democrat and the Northeast and much of the Midwest supported his Republican opponent.

In 1920, 1924 and 1928 a series of Republican candidates won the Presidential elections in all cases winning the Northeast and most of the rest of the country but with the South determinedly opposed. A change would come in 1932.

The sectional pattern of American politics—a Republican Northeast and a Democrat South—had endured from 1856 until 1932—76 years. Then the Great Depression precipitated a reversal of sectional political allegiances—a pirouette of our political parties—one of the most remarkable transitions in politics anytime, anywhere.

The Pirouette of the Political Parties

Introducing confusion into the sectional character of American politics is the remarkable pirouette of our political parties. Over the past 100 years the pirouette has placed the Republicans in the geographic position once occupied by the Democrats, and the Democrats in the position once occupied by the Republicans.

After the Civil War, for decades the North was solidly Republican and the South was solidly Democratic. People spoke of the Republicans as the "Grand Old Party," (the "GOP") and meant that it was the epitome of the Northern political orientation. People spoke of "the solid South," referring to the predictable entry of every Southern state into the Democratic column in Presidential elections.

Until 1932 the sectional division of the United States between the two major political parties was firm and unchanging except at the margin. The Northeast voted Republican; the South voted Democrat. Elections were determined by the swing states of the Border, the Midwest, the Mountain states and the Pacific coast.

But the election of 1932 altered the pattern. The Great Depression had begun in 1929 and 1932 was the first presidential election after the Depression had begun. The Democratic candidate, Franklin Roosevelt carried the entire country except for five states in the Northeast, which remained stubbornly Republican. The Depression had trumped sectionalism and pushed it into the background. There it remained for the next three presidential elections—all of which FDR won. The whole country appeared to be leaning Democrat; Republicans seemed to be on the verge of extinction.

The Great Depression was the time in which the large unions emerged, and FDR made them solidly Democratic. Southern Democrats found themselves uncomfortably in the same political party as their economic enemies—unionists. Similarly, the unionists of the Northeast and Midwest were uncomfortable with their Southern conservative political allies.

The victory of the Democratic Party in five straight Presidential elections beginning in 1932 and ending in 1948 (when the Democrats won for the last time in that sequence) were made possible by the remarkable coalition of the formerly Confederate states, conservative and strongly racist, and the Northern states in which labor unions and minority groups who were liberal or progressive dominated the Democratic Party and slowly weakened the grip of the GOP on the Northeast

The sectional complexion of national politics was visible again after the end of Democratic dominance. In 1952 Republicans led by Dwight Eisenhower recaptured almost all the country, except for most of the South which continued stubbornly Democrat. In 1956 Eisenhower won reelection again losing only the South (and even then some Southern states voted for Ike).

In 1960 the usual sectional pattern seemed extinct. Jack Kennedy carried the South and the Northeast, losing most of the Midwest, the Mountain states and the Pacific West. The Northeast had voted Democrat again. FDR had made the Northeast safe for Democrats, ending the Republican ascendancy that had prevailed since the Civil War.

During and immediately after the Great Depression the liberal wing of the Democratic Party had grown in political power. It was centered in the Northeast. It had elected John Kennedy president.

In the aftermath of Kennedy's assassination, Lyndon Johnson, a Texas Democrat, became president. Johnson leaned heavily toward the social agenda of the northern and liberal wing of the Democratic Party. A voting rights bill was proposed to bring more minority voters to the polls in the South.

A reaction occurred almost immediately in the Deep South. Johnson was elected in his own right in 1964 carrying all the country except the Deep South, which for the first time voted Republican. The solidly Democratic South which had preceded the Civil War and continued for more than 100 years disappeared.

In 1965 Lyndon Johnson signed into law an act intended to change the politics of the South from conservative to liberal. This was the Voting Rights Act. When signing the law, Johnson commented that it meant that the Democrats would lose the South in national elections for a generation. Johnson was correct in direction, but not in timing. In fact, the law meant that the Democrats would lose the South for several generations— perhaps indefinitely. The South saw the law as a return to Reconstruction, except this time minority votes in the South would be used to entrench in national office Northern Democrats instead of Northern Republicans. The law was intended to favor liberal Democrats in the South, thereby changing the political complexion of the South from conservative to liberal, while retaining its orientation to the Democratic Party. Instead, the South remained conservative, but changed parties.

To a large degree the shift of political allegiance in the South was a direct response to the shift of political allegiance in the Northeast. But the shift of the South to the Republicans was not without second thoughts. In the election of 1968 the South refused to back either Republicans or Democrats, voting instead for a third, Southern party. Richard Nixon, the Republican, was elected by majorities everywhere else except the Northeast which now demonstrated that it was securely Democratic.

In 1972 the Democrats ran George McGovern for the presidency, a candidate so unpopular that again sectional political divisions were masked as they had been in FDR's time. In 1972 the Republicans carried virtually the entire country including the Northeast (except for Massachusetts).

In 1976 the Democrats made a bid to recapture the allegiance of the South by running the governor of Georgia for the presidency. Again, sectional divisions were obscured when Jimmy Carter won the presidency. Generally speaking, the Democrats won the east of the country and the presidency; the Republicans won the west of the country and lost the presidency. This was a repeat of the election of 1960 in that the country seemed to be divided sectionally between east and west.

In 1980 Jimmy Carter was so unpopular that he united the country against his reelection, carrying only Georgia and a few states in other sections of the country.

Ronald Reagan won reelection in 1984 with majorities in virtually the entire country. There seemed to be no sectional divide in our politics. At this point many Americans forgot about the sectional division and presumed that the legacy of the Civil War was fully eliminated.

The election of 1992 seemed to confirm that judgment. The Republican candidate was reelected with majorities in all sections.

But in 1992 and 1996 sectionalism reasserted itself in a surprising context. The governor of a Southern state, Bill Clinton of Arkansas, ran for president as a Democrat and was elected and reelected. Yet most of the South voted Republican against him. This was a surprise. Running a Southern governor for president no longer assured the Democrats of electoral victories in the South.

In 2000 and 2004 a former governor of Texas, George W. Bush, won election and reelection, carrying the South and losing the Northeast in both elections. The usual sectional pattern was back.

In 2008 and 2012 the usual sectional pattern asserted itself strongly. The Democrat candidate Barack Obama carried the Northeast and lost most of the South, but carried Virginia and Florida each time. Virginia's position as a border state was confirmed.

The Period 1932 to 2000 Was Not a New Normal for American National Politics But Was Only an Interlude

The pirouette of the political parties was complete. The Northeast was now determinedly Democrat; the South was as determinedly Republican. The period from 1932 to 2000 was revealed as largely an interlude in which the transitional shifting of the political parties concealed the continuing sectionalism at the heart of American politics.

FDR had created for the Democratic Party a winning political coalition out of Northern liberals and Southern conservatives. He had held the odd couple together for more than a decade. The political marriage outlived him by more than 50 years. It took several decades for the Southern Democrats to break-up the odd marriage by turning themselves into Republicans. By 2000, the adjustment had been made and America was as sectionally divided as before, but with the political complexion reversed in the two sections.

Within a few election cycles Democrats had replaced Republicans as the dominant national political party in the Northeast. In the South Republicans had displaced Democrats as the dominant political party. Unfortunately for the Democrats, what they gained in the Northeast they lost in the South. Unfortunately for the Republicans, as they gained in the South, they lost in the Northeast. The old sectional division of the United States in the Civil War demonstrated its continuing domination of American politics. In the aftermath of the political pirouette of the parties, the South was no longer Democrat but was now Republican, and the Northeast was no longer Republican but now Democrat. The gulf between North and South remained—unchanged except for political labels.

The shift in party alignment in the two sections had significant impact on local and state politics and upon the careers of individual politicians. This is a reason the realignments took several decades to complete. In the Northeast white, Anglo-Saxon Protestant families had dominated Republican politics. A WASP (FDR) led the shift to the Democrats, and after him the sons and daughters of recent immigrants, largely southern European and Catholic, dominated the Democrat Party. This is one of the reasons there was such deep bitterness against FDR in many Republican households in the Northeast. A man from a wealthy family, Roosevelt appeared to many as a traitor to his economic class. But equally or more important, he was a WASP who appeared to open the door to political power in the Northeast to Catholics. He had, that is, promoted a demographic shift in power.

Northeastern WASPs were marginalized politically—they became people with strong political opinions but little political power. (The one possible exception is George H. W. Bush, scion of an old Republican WASP political family in Connecticut and elected President of the United States in 1988. But his election was largely due to his previous role as vice-president for Ronald Reagan, a California not a Northeast Republican, and George H. W. Bush lost reelection in 1992.)

In the South, many conservative Democrats switched parties, so that the traditional leadership of the South remained intact but with different party labels. Thus it is that today many Southern Republicans recall without rancor that their parents were Roosevelt Democrats.

The sectional differentiation in the politics of America is as visible today as it has ever been. The Northeast aligns with one party; the South with the other. Border States and the Midwest are as much the primary swing states as they were at the time of the Civil War

—sometimes voting Republican and sometimes Democratic. It is worth recalling that the reason there was a bitter Civil War was that the South gained the support of the most significant of the Border States, Virginia. Without Virginia, the Confederacy was not viable. And the reason the North prevailed in the Civil War was that it was able to gain and hold the allegiance of the Midwestern states. Without the support of the Midwest the Northeast could not have won the Civil War. The Border and Midwestern states still today hold the balance of power in American politics.

It is of great significance that the legacy of the War continues in our politics. All American presidential elections are in a sense a re-contest of the American Civil War.

Sectionalism is not the only thing going on in American national politics, of course. In some presidential elections it is not the most important thing. Sometimes dominant issues of personalities act to submerge the sectional division. But sectionalism that reflects the issues over which the Civil War was fought never disappears from our national politics and in many elections reasserts itself as the dominant factor.

Most of our presidential elections boil down to a contest in which most states and electoral votes have already been determined on a sectional basis and the contest is narrowed down to a few "swing" states. This is the ordinary dynamic of presidential elections and it makes the sectional orientation of our political parties the most important influence in American national politics.

CHAPTER EIGHT

The Hinge of American Politics Turns Between the Northeast and South

The fact that there is a sectional hinge around which swings American presidential politics is a consequence of the centuries long effort of the Northeast, generally successful, to impose its economic and social preferences on the rest of the country. The Civil War perpetuated the economic, social and political dominance of the United States by the Northeast that continues to this day.

The Contest Between Northeast and South

Why is the sectional dynamic so significant in American national politics? What underlies it?

American national politics have been dominated since the Civil War by the Northeast, first in the form of the Republican Party and more recently in the form of the Democratic Party.

From the perspective of critics of the Northeastern elite, the hinge around which American politics turns is the unending effort of the Northeastern states to impose economic and social policies which they favor on the rest of the country. Some historians have traced this back to the Puritan-Royalist conflict of the English Civil War and have seen it as a contest between capitalism (commerce) and aristocratic forms of government and economic life (i.e., manorial or plantation).

It has made no difference in the past 160 years whether the Northeast acted via the Republican Party as it did for most of the 19th century, or via the Democratic Party as it has acted more recently. Furthermore, over time the economic and social preferences of the Northeast have evolved. For example, at the end of World War I Northeastern Republicans led the political effort to keep the United States out of the League of Nations—a Northeastern agenda item which was conservative in nature. Today Northeastern Democrats (now the dominant political party in the region) are major supporters of the League's successor, the United Nations—a Northeastern agenda item which is liberal in nature. So, the Northeast switched from an isolationist preference to an internationalist preference, and, of course, expected the rest of the country to switch with it—which it largely did.

Paul Freund, a long-time professor at the Harvard Law School, explained the political dynamic most clearly (see "Unity and Diversity: Changing Meanings," in Henry F. Thomas, ed., *The American Prospect*, Boston: Houghton Mifflin, 1977). His is a clear statement of the Northeast liberal's view of American history and its progress. He begins by praising the compromises made to get the Constitution adopted, although these included acceptance of slavery in the South. He then praises the actions of Chief Justice Marshall that consolidated power in the Federal government, permitting the Northeast to press its economic agenda of tariffs to support manufacturing and infrastructure improvements to link the Northeast with the Midwest. Then he endorses the Civil War and the 1960s court decisions which imposed the Northeast social agenda on the entire country.

In essence, Freund described a political dynamic in which the Northeastern states first established a central government and then exploited the government to impose its agenda on the rest of the country. Because the Northeast does not have a majority of the nation's population, its success required the consent of a portion of the rest of the country. Generally the Northeast has acquired enough support in the rest of the country to achieve a majority in the Congress and control of the presidency. The imposition of the Northeastern agenda was done by legislation, court decisions, actions of the executive and, in the case of the Civil War, by war.

Resentment and resistance in the South to the Northeastern agenda is also an enduring theme in American politics, splitting the country along sectional lines. As the country expanded to its current 50 states, the far West became allied politically with the Northeast, while the Border States, the Midwest and Mountain states swung in support of the Northeast sometimes and of the South at other times. The continuing success of the Northeast in gaining support in the Midwest in order to press its agenda is the more impressive because of the Northeast's steady loss in the last 50 years of population and Congressional representation to the South and West.

A Legacy of Distrust

The Northeast-South division is not the only sectional division in the United States. There are other sectional divisions, for example, between the West Coast and the East Coast and between the coasts and the interior of the country. There are also non-sectional divisions which have significance; for example, between urban dwellers and suburban or rural residents; between progressives and traditionalists; between Christians and atheists; among the various ethnic groups, etc. But none of these groups have ever fought wars with each other; and in none of these divisions is there the depth of dislike and bitterness that has resulted between Northeast and South as a consequence of the Civil War.

In general, the elite of the Northeast describe Southerners as ignorant and culturally backward; the elite of the South view Northeasterners as hypocritical busybodies. Northeasterners have contempt for most Southerners but don't dwell on the matter. Southerners often conceal bitter resentment behind a false veneer of courtesy, so that Northeasterners are generally unaware of it.

Southern resentment comes directly from the Civil War and its aftermath—from invasion and devastation and a century of impoverishment for the section as a whole. It also comes from the attitude of moral superiority assumed by Northeasterners with respect to other Americans. At least, that is how most Southerners view the matter.

In recent decades many Northerners have moved to the South. Those who have located in Northeastern enclaves in the South, such as exist in southern and middle Florida, generally have retained their Northeastern attitudes. Those who have settled in areas in which Northeasterners are a minority have often acquired Southern attitudes.

In general, Southerners resent the New York elite and distrust Northeasterners ("Yankees") generally. Resentment is nourished continually by media reports and personal experiences of the arrogance and dishonesty of the financial elite.

Resentment is not limited to Southerners. People all over the country have lost pensions and health insurance, often their jobs as well, in the process of reorganization of firms taken over by private equity firms operating primarily out of the Northeast. Bankers have foreclosed on people's homes; credit ratings have deprived people of borrowing opportunities. The major banks are Northeastern. Resentment is deep and bitter. But it is rarely openly expressed. People understand who runs the country, and fear those people.

Ordinary people appear afraid that if they express resentment, they will lose their jobs or see their credit ratings fall, or be denied loans, or have their homes foreclosed on, or have problems with the Internal Revenue Service—all of which have happened in the past few years. It doesn't matter that whether a Democrat or a Republican is in the White House; people seem to understand that both political parties are largely subservient to the financial power that is centered in the Northeast, though many Southerners are trying to deny influence in the Republican Party to Northeastern-based banks, hedge funds and private equity funds.

A discussion at a dinner party held in the summer of 2013 is instructive.

"Everyone I know in the South hates New Yorkers," a man observed.

"Do you hate them yourself?" he was asked.

"I live in New York City," he answered, neatly side-stepping the question. "But I grew up in the South and I visit there frequently. People tell me the truth about how they feel because they think I'm one of them."

"Hate is a strong word," another guest at the table observed. "Wouldn't it be more accurate to say that Southerners dislike or distrust Yankees?"

"I don't think dislike is strong enough. I know New Yorkers don't like to think that many other Americans hate them, but they do. Most people won't say so publicly because they fear New Yorkers. My only reservation," the man continued, "is that hate is not a strong enough term." He paused, letting the significance of his comments sink in. Then he added, "New Yorkers are especially hated because they represent the economic oppression of the South that began soon after the nation was formed and continues today."

A charitable view of this matter recognizes that there are millions of New Yorkers and as individuals they vary greatly. Some are kind and caring and polite; others are vicious. This is true of all groups of people. Many non-New Yorkers have close friends who are New Yorkers and esteem them highly. It is as a political and financial group that New Yorkers become intolerable to many other Americans. As a group the majority of New Yorkers seem to their opponents to be arrogant, dissembling, greedy, intolerant, grasping and hypocritical.

Opinion polls and focus groups don't suggest a wide degree of resentment of the Northeast. But many respondents may be so frightened of the power of the Northeast that polls and focus groups will not reveal the actual depth of feeling. Respondents don't trust pollsters and focus group leaders to be truly independent of the financial and political reach of the Northeast. But the depth of feeling is evident in the distaste which many people have expressed for Presidents John F. Kennedy and Barack Obama, each of whom is to them a symbol of Northeastern power.

Deep resentment is rarely expressed outside the safe circles of relatives and friends. This seems to be for fear of retaliation by the North. If retaliation should be dismissed as farfetched, one might rethink. This is an age of speech control—of political correctness and legal prosecution for outlying expressions or even jokes. A person inclined to doubt this might try joking at a security check point in an airport. Some expressions for which people are condemned in the media and threatened with legal prosecution are called "hate" words, and what is more a hate word that the expression of hate itself? Cautious Southerners use words like "dislike" when speaking of their emotions toward New Yorkers.

Before the Civil War, there was in the South rivalry with Northerners generally and dislike for abolitionists. But it was rivalry and dislike, not bitter resentment. But the experience of war made the emotion deeper.

Fear of the Central Government

Fear of the federal government—a legacy not only of the Revolution but of the Civil War—may be at the heart of the controversy over gun control in America—though this is never acknowledged by the mainstream media.

The Second Amendment reads in pertinent part: "the right of the people to keep and bear Arms, shall not be infringed." It is ordinarily presumed in the media and in elite opinion in the Northeast and West Coast that people who want to have guns have as motivation either fear of criminals or a sort of irrational foolishness —that they are red—necks or yahoos. There is much more to it than that.

A great many Americans fear our federal government. For some it is a legacy of the Revolution. Any strong, centralized government—like that of Britain at the time of the Revolution—is a source of fear to people who value their independence and autonomy greatly.

For others fear of the federal government is a result of the strong centralized government that has emerged in America during and since the Civil War—a central government that leaves state and local authorities little scope. Many people seem to fear a centralized government that is armed to the teeth—including an enormous standing army, National Guard units, and state and local police forces of great number, professionalism and weaponry—all of which are subject to federal control in emergencies.

To a large degree fear of the government is one of the shadows left by the Civil War. In the South fear of a Northern-dominated federal government is a direct result of the War; in the rest of the country it is an indirect result of the centralization and apparent ruthlessness of the government which originated in the War. The federal government during the Civil War demonstrated that it would suspend civil liberties as necessary and that it would destroy homes and livelihoods on a massive scale to prevail over disgruntled citizens.

Possibly, many Americans want guns and the protection of the Second Amendment for potential use in a crisis against the government. When the Mayor of New York City and the President of the United States call for gun control, many people hear the voice of an over-armed, over-violent government threatening their lives and freedoms by removing their last line of defense.

Distrust and fear of the federal government should not be thought to be limited to people who live in the states of the old Confederacy. Americans from all states are mobile. Many people in the Midwest and Far West are fearful of the federal government. Armed confrontations between ranchers and federal authorities have occurred in recent years.

In addition, Southerners moving from the old Confederacy to other states carry with them their fears and resentments. In conversations they influence others with their attitudes. Hence, a residue of the Civil War continues to motivate many Americans all over the country to seek protection from the violence of federal authorities by arming themselves.

In recent years Americans have seen the overwhelming armed force with which federal authorities stamp out the lives of people accused (not convicted ordinarily) of violating law. For example, in the spring of 1993, after a 51-day siege of a compound in Waco, Texas, the FBI launched an assault in which 76 men, women, and children died. The important thing was the slaughter, since many Americans (if not most) recognized that the victims might or might not have been guilty of violating any laws.

Keeping pistols and rifles would probably be of no real value in resisting attack by federal authorities including the military (as occurred in Waco). But that observation only makes people want more lethal weapons—such as semi- and automatic firing weapons. People would often prefer to be able to defend themselves, even though they are likely to be subdued in the end.

It may seem ironic, or even inconsistent, that many people who are pro-gun in part because of fear of the federal government are also among our strongest patriots. We might wonder how they can combine their desire to harbor arms against a government they fear along with their support (in most cases) of a strong national defense. Contradictions in politics are everywhere, but this apparent anomaly is among the more fascinating ones in our country.

In summary, the penchant of many Americans for the possession of guns seems not merely for the purpose of protecting themselves from crime. It seems equally or more for the protection of themselves from excessive use of power by the federal government. This concern antedates the American Revolution and was increased by the Civil War.

The more Northeasterners and their supporters elsewhere in the country call for gun control, the more suspicious many Americans become of their motives and the more concerned for their own safety. Hence, whenever federal authorities and the media press for new gun control legislation, the sales of guns and ammunition jump dramatically. After each unsuccessful effort at additional gun control, Americans are more fully armed than before.

Northeasterners and their supporters seem to not understand this political dynamic. They express astonishment that anyone would resist efforts at gun control. After all, they insist, why would anyone want to endorse killing sprees by deranged individuals of bystanders and children such as occur from time to time in America? Their astonishment seems sincere. They attribute resistance to proposals to increase gun control legislation to ignorance more than anything else. Since the Northeast and its allies control the American media, many people abroad adopt the attitudes of the Northeast and believe that people who oppose gun control legislation are merely ignorant. It never seems to occur to them that the people of the United States might want to be armed against the excesses of their own federal government.

This discussion is about a secondary culture of the United States. A minority within a demographic majority—people who do not accept the generally accepted interpretation of the history and politics of the country—people who sometimes hold political power nationally, and in some states are almost continuously in power, yet are nevertheless a form of counterculture politically. In much discussion of America, these people are simply ignored; or they are dismissed as a lunatic fringe. Beaten they have been and usually are—both by physical force and in elections—but they constitute an undeniable and continuing undercurrent in American politics and society—an undercurrent which affects the direction of America and may in the future become dominant.

To these people and others less marginalized, perhaps in total a majority of Americans, the federal government under control of the Northeast and its allies is the essence of arbitrary rule. The government seems willing to jail or kill people who disagree with its preferences—which are always presented as moral principles. If one doesn't accept the popular culture with its tacit support of drugs, sex, and violence; if one doesn't embrace the political aspirations of the Civil Rights Movement; if one resists feminist ambitions; if one opposes abortion; if one rejects the gay life style; if one speaks outside the bounds of political correctness; then one is subject to the full weight of the government's discipline; sometimes without legislative permission but merely by administrative action—which is the essence of arbitrary government; and if people oppose the demands of the government, it will use military force to kill them, as it did in the Civil War and at Waco.

Public opinion polls give little or no indication of such attitudes existing in any significant part of the population. It will probably be asserted that the overwhelming majority of Americans trust their federal government and would never think of arming themselves against it. Only a fringe of neo-Nazis have such attitudes, it will be said. But of course, if a person distrusts the federal government and the media as fully as many Americans appear to do, then they will never acknowledge that to pollsters, government officials or politicians. And our politicians, now overwhelmingly attorneys in their training, are not trusted by our people anyway, as poll after poll shows.

Finally, it might be objected that people who will tell pollsters that they distrust politicians should have no hesitation about telling pollsters that they distrust government. This objection has merit, though many Americans do tell pollsters that they distrust not only politicians but government. Nonetheless, it's one thing to tell a pollster you distrust politicians, when most other Americans are doing the same. It may seem a different thing entirely—and much more risky—to tell the police and military power that you distrust it, when few others are willing to do so and when you believe, as many Americans seem to, that the government will identify and retaliate against you.

It seems a dangerous thing for a person to tell pollsters that she or he distrusts government in the context of the controversy over gun control—implying that a person wants weapons for possible use against the government itself. Who knows how the government might respond? So people seem to keep cautiously quiet.

People who fear the federal government are also people who feel themselves powerless to affect that government's decisions or actions. Most Americans report to pollsters that they feel that way. Powerless in the face of what seems arbitrary rule, many people seem to want whatever protection weapons can supply and are cautious to conceal from the government and its supporters their motivations.

Incidentally, fear of possible oppression by the federal government does not mean that people opt out of national public life. Some do; most don't. People who fear the federal government may still vote, have opinions on national issues, and support the federal government in many things that it does domestically and abroad. This may seem inconsistent, but it should not be surprising. It happens in many countries all over the world.

Could the United States Divide Again?

Some people in the South, the Midwest and the Mountain States would leave the United States politically if they could do it peacefully. They would do so in order to escape what they see as Wall Street's avarice and Washington's corruption. Could there be another division of the country?

While another division of the nation on a sectional basis is highly unlikely, there is a context in which the United States might divide.

It is a disputed election which cannot be resolved. This possibility appeared in the election of 2000 in which only the willingness, even impatient desire of the Democrat candidate Al Gore, to lose the election prevented a Constitutional crisis. Such a crisis would have occurred, if when the Supreme Court effectively declared George W. Bush the winner of the presidential election, Al Gore had refused to concede and President Bill Clinton had supported Gore. President Clinton might have said to the Supreme Court, "Enforce your own orders." The Court has no ability to enforce its own orders. This is a formulation which several American presidents have used in the past when they were in conflict with the Supreme Court. So such an action by President Clinton would not have been unprecedented, though its application to the outcome of a Presidential election would have been unprecedented. Had Gore refused to concede, and had President Clinton supported him, the resulting Constitutional crisis would have threatened to break the country apart on the traditional lines of South (which had voted for Bush) versus Northeast (which had voted for Gore) with the rest of the country having to choose sides.

In the Northeast any possibility of disunion is rejected out of hand. The lesson of the Civil War remains alive—the country cannot be dismembered. But the South is not so sure. Many things are thought to be different now. Perhaps a division is possible.

When the Governor of Texas reminded Americans in 2013 that Texas reserves its right (allegedly included in the act by which Texas voluntarily entered the Union in 1845) to leave the United States, Northerners presumed he was joking. Southerners knew that instead he was articulating a deeply held and infrequently expressed desire in the hearts of many Southerners. This does not mean that Southerners are seeking at this moment the dissolution of the United States. They understand that that is impossible. The federal government is far too strong—it is far too well armed—for any serious effort at dissolution to succeed.

PART FOUR

The War Changed America's Relationship to the Rest of the World

CHAPTER NINE

In the Civil War America Became Committed to Remaking Other Societies in its Own Image

A key purpose of the Civil War was to remake the South in the image of the North politically, economically and socially. The effort was largely successful. As a result Americans generally believe that they can remake other societies in their own image. Today the United States is frequently engaged in nation-building activities abroad—many of which are failures.

The Ups and Downs of Nation-Building

In the aftermath of the Civil War the American people got the notion that their country was able to remake entire societies. During the Reconstruction decade which followed the war, the North effectively changed the Southern states forever. Slavery and all hopes of restoring it were eliminated in the South. Also eliminated were all expectations of an independent South—not the wish for it, which continued in many hearts, whether or not slavery could have been restored, but the expectation that it could be achieved. As a result, Southerners reentered the United States providing a disproportionate share of its military personnel and playing a vigorous role in its political, and later economic, life. So the South had been remade. In modern parlance, there had been what appeared on the surface to have been successful nation-building by the Union in the defeated states of the South.

Puritan settlers of New England had brought to the New World the notion of building a society that would be a model for the world. "A city built on a hill," they called it, borrowing a phrase from the Bible. But until the Civil War, the spread of the New England model had been attempted by peaceful example; after the Civil War it would frequently be done by force.

Encouraged by successful nation-building in the South after the Civil War, the United States embarked after World War II on a nation-building effort in Japan. There was great success. A democracy replaced the old imperial system and the militarism of pre-war Japan was extinguished. Again, nation-building was successful.

It is perhaps not surprising, therefore, that the United States would attempt several times again to replicate its earlier successes in nation-building. Efforts were made in South Vietnam, Iraq and Afghanistan. Building a viable nation in South Vietnam failed. In Iraq and Afghanistan Americans tried to build modern democratic societies. We attempted to liberate women from traditional roles and restraints, rather as slaves had been liberated during our Civil War. But in Iraq and Afghanistan liberation and nation-building efforts appear to have largely failed.

The American Cycle of Militarism and Pacifism

The South was restructured by the North via military conquest. No real effort was made to win the hearts and minds of the South; the effort was to so far intimidate Southerners by force that they would cease to resist and accept the political and social make-over which the North imposed. It worked. Hence, we have come to rely increasingly on military power to achieve our political aims in the world.

Power matters; it can cause things to get done. During the American Civil War the French government, under the pretext of collecting unpaid debts in Mexico, sent troops to occupy that country. The French overthrew the Mexican Republic and established a monarchy and placed on the throne of Mexico a Hapsburg prince. This was in American eyes a clear violation of the Monroe Doctrine, but the United States was too busy with its Civil War to take action. Meanwhile, another war in Mexico, between the French and Mexicans, occurred. When the American Civil War ended, the United States immediately sent 50,000 troops under one of the Union's best generals to the Mexican border. At this time the United States possessed the world's largest, best led, best equipped, and most experienced army—the accompaniment of the Union's victory in the Civil War. The United States also possessed the world's most up-to-date Navy. The French understood the threat from the United States and immediately withdrew their troops from Mexico. Their puppet government collapsed and Mexican republicans took over Mexico again.

From a certain perspective, the United States displays a remarkable cycle of military aggressiveness and passivity. At times the US engages in war—some of which it initiates. At other times the US disarms. After the Civil War the United States largely disarmed until the Spanish-American War. After World War I, the United States disarmed again. At the time the United States entered World War II, for example, it ranked about 15th in the world in military power, behind Bulgaria. But at the end of the Second World War the United States was, as it remains today, the strongest military power on the planet.

The U.S. learned in the Civil War that military power can resolve difficult issues—by military force the Northern states held together the Union and eliminated slavery. It was by force that these two objectives were achieved, though it is conceivable that both might have been achieved peacefully under a different President. Thereafter, the United States destroyed the Spanish Empire by military force. It helped crush German aspirations to world power twice in the 20th century; and the United States drove Japan back into its islands. By military power the United States frustrated the ambitions of the Soviet Union. By military power it now attempts to frustrate the ambitions of China, the Islamists and Russia.

Americans learned in the Civil War the great potential of military force for pursuit of American objectives and have not yet renounced or forgotten the lesson. At this moment the United States seems to be in the militaristic stage of its cycle between militarism and pacifism. But it seems likely that we may be beginning to turn again toward pacifism.

The Current American Confusion about Nation-Building

America appears to have ended up at a point of confusion in its efforts at nation-building. We rely on military force, but we don't wish to do that. So we limit the use of force, trying to avoid injuring or frightening our adversaries' civilians and providing opportunities for enemy combatants to withdraw from fighting. This is the notion of winning hearts and minds. But it isn't clear that coupling such efforts at peaceful persuasion is successful when accompanied by a military campaign.

American leadership in recent decades has ignored the stringent requirements for success in nation-building that were met with respect to the Southern states and Japan. United States' forces occupied its two enemies (roughly four decades apart), utterly crushed all armed opposition, attempted to persuade the civilian population by what we would call today terror that resistance was useless, took over the governments entirely (for years after the end of World War II, American General Douglas MacArthur ruled Japan), and imposed whatever changes were desired by the American authorities.

This pattern has not been followed since. Instead, American forces have strictly restricted the application of military power in the apparent conviction that winning the hearts and minds of enemy populations was feasible. This was a major change in strategy. Not the hearts and minds of the Southern population nor those of the Japanese were won by Americans during the wars involved, and probably haven't been won even today. The Japanese as well as Southerners have great but well concealed resentment of the United States. American force made way for nation-building.

In Vietnam, Iraq and Afghanistan, American troops performed a limited occupation role and attempted to prevent civilian casualties (though, of course, some did occur). Local governments, even if dependent on the American presence, were given substantial discretion and independence.

When we were dealing with the South during and after the Civil War and with Japan during and after World War II, we used overwhelming military force during the wars and took direct control of the government after the wars in both instances. In this way we won total victory and found that we could then redesign the societies to fit our own preferences. Further, we could banish conflict with them for long periods—perhaps for an indefinite future. But when we came recently to Vietnam, Iraq and Afghanistan, we decided we needed to earn hearts and minds by restraint in the use of force, only to discover that we then failed in our overall objectives—in particular in nation-building. So it wasn't the effort to nation-build that was at fault—we did that successfully after the Civil War and World War II—but that we couldn't achieve the preconditions for nation-building. Either the precondition involves overwhelming use of force, which we have not done, or it is winning hearts and minds, which we have failed to do in conjunction with the use of force. We had somehow changed our basic approach from the Civil War and World War II into the period of limited wars of the late 20th and early 21st centuries, and in doing so we lost our ability to rebuild nations in our own image.

It appears that the American government has retained the memory of success in nation-building but has forgotten how it was achieved and hasn't fashioned a new way that is successful. The result is that the American reach exceeds its grasp in the world today—that is, the United States employs force to facilitate nation-building but is not able to achieve its objectives—and a result is frustration and tragedy for all involved.

Human Rights Have Displaced Imperialism as a Cause for American Intervention Abroad

The Civil War was in large part an exercise in the advancement of human rights.

The United States had, however, both before and after the Civil War experimented with European-style imperialism as a motive for interventions abroad. The Mexican War was in many ways such a war early in the 19th century; and the Spanish-American War was such a war at the end of the 19th century.

Many Americans were uncomfortable with imperial motivation, and World War I, World War II, the Korean War, the Vietnam War and the two Iraqi Wars were fought for motivations of defense—at least as stated by the Administrations involved.

But in the Afghan War we returned to the Civil War precedent of human rights as a justification for intervention and the use of force, and are have been doing so in interventions, even if not full-scale war, in many parts of the world.

There are those who insist that human rights are not a real motivation, but rather a cover for commercial purposes, as was partly the case in the Civil War. But this only makes the comparison with the Civil War tighter. In the Civil War, as we have seen, motives of human rights accompanied those of commercial interest.

For those many Americans whose motivations in intervening in conflicts abroad are humanitarian, or to support human rights, the purposes are exemplary. But there is often great human suffering associated with military interventions, and many interventions do not end in permanent improvements for the peoples involved.

The process is the same—military intervention and political control—whatever the motivation. But the common rationale has been shifted from imperialism (rejected by modern political thinking), and defense (recently overused in the Second Iraqi War and the Afghan War) to protection of human rights. This is a rationale which is championed by modern political thinking, just as it was championed by the thinking of the Civil War period, when war as a means to enhance human rights gained a strong foothold in American thinking.

CHAPTER TEN

In the Civil War America Decided to Make War on Civilian Populations

Toward the end of the Civil War key Union generals explicitly targeted Southern civilians and their property in an effort to terrorize the civilian population into such panic that the Confederate government would surrender. America continued that strategy in World War II on a massive scale. The assault on civilians during the Civil War left lasting resentment in the South and did little to win the war. The same was true of the effort in World War II.

There have been many times in history during which civilians have been attacked during war. For much of history a purpose of war was to capture civilians for enslavement. Sometimes a purpose of war was to destroy a city or a nation, and civilians were killed or enslaved as part of the objective. This was true of the Roman destruction of Carthage and of the Mongol conquest of India.

Throughout history, blood-maddened soldiers who had stormed cities often robbed, raped and murdered civilians. This continued on a large scale in the 20th century. Japanese soldiers carried out massive atrocities in China during the Japanese invasion of China in the 1930s and 1940s; Soviet soldiers did the same in Germany as World War II drew to an end.

But as civilization advanced, this became less common. By the 17th and 18th centuries in Europe, wars were sometimes waged with the civilian population generally untouched. In America, the wars between European settlers and Native Americans often involved the massacre of civilian populations and destruction of homes and settlements. But leaders on both sides frequently descried this and attempted to limit the savagery.

The Civil War began with commendable restraint on both sides. Civilians were largely untouched. Northern armies marching through the South were frequently denounced by Southern non-combatants without reprisal, and the same thing happened when Southern armies marched North. A poem celebrates an older woman who leaned out a window and shouted to Confederate soldiers who were marching through the streets of her Northern town:

"Shoot if you must this old grey head,

But spare your country's flag, she said."

She was not shot.

Though there were civilian casualties in warfare throughout history, they were not normally part of a programmatic effort by a government to terrorize the civilian population of an adversary into surrender. Terrorize is the right word. It is the word used by writers in the 1920s and 1930s who urged combatant nations to use aerial bombing to terrorize the civilian populations of adversary nations into surrender. It never worked, as careful studies of strategic bombing after the war indicated, including a study in which John Kenneth Galbraith took a leading part. But in the case of Japan, the atomic bombs combined with conventional fire-bombing of Japanese cities provided the Japanese emperor with a rationale to end the war by surrender. Perhaps this was a form of ultimate success for terror attacks on civilian populations.

The strategic purpose of a civilized modern nation to make war on a civilian population was started by Grant, Sherman and Sheridan (each of whom gave voice to it) and was approved by Lincoln. Sherman put the threat most clearly: "A people who will persevere in war beyond a certain limit ought to know the consequences. Many, many peoples with less pertinacity have been wiped out of national existence." And even more concisely, "I will make Georgia howl!" These were not threats directed at the Southern fighting men, but at their families.

The Union political and military leadership adopted the principle that a good end can justify the means used to attain it. In their view, it was permissible to do wrong in a good cause. The principle has since been adopted by American governments on important occasions.

In the Civil War one saw for the first time the Northern predilection for war without limit —moral or physical—said to be justified by the end—again the end justifying the means. This predilection became very pronounced in the Second World War with the bombing of civilian populations in Europe and the use of atomic weapons on Japan. Since the Civil War the U.S. has sometimes adopted a terror war doctrine—terror employed against enemy civilian populations by burning and bombing from the air.

Terror need not be associated with "total" war. This is a necessary distinction. Total war refers to the mobilization of an entire nation for the waging of war. It is a term used in contrast to "limited war." Ordinarily, total war is not associated with the employment of all means of death and destruction against an enemy. It is possible to prosecute total war without intentionally slaughtering enemy civilians.

We have in recent years confused this discussion by using the term "terrorism" for a sort of guerrilla war, and by promulgating a "War on Terror." Guerrilla wars are now common, and America often gets involved. In such wars it is difficult to separate combatants from civilians, especially where guerrillas do not want to be separated from the surrounding civilian population. In such wars civilian casualties are common, though American forces in recent years seem to have minimized their occurrence even at the cost of higher casualties to our soldiers.

Terror war is a different notion. It involves assaulting enemy civilians in the belief that terror and destruction will cause the enemy to cease fighting. It is a cold blooded strategy adopted for a purpose and pursued with relentless savagery. It involves the intentional dispossession and slaughter of civilians as an act of terror. America has employed terror war almost exclusively in the prosecution of major warfare—especially in World War II.

Terror war is very different from a one-time attack on civilians by soldiers in the heat of battle; it is also very different from civilian casualties which occur without intention in a guerrilla (or anti-terrorism) type war. Practiced as America has practiced it in the past, by bombing from the air, it has no element of passion—whether for revenge or military advantage; it is cold-minded.

The terrorization of the Southern population during the Civil War was primarily accomplished by destroying homes, towns, cities and food supplies. There is little evidence of the slaughter of civilians on a large scale, though many Southerners, especially women and children—since men were often away in the armies—died either in burning buildings, by weapons wielded by Union soldiers or camp followers, or by starvation after the Union armies had passed.

Sherman's impoverishment of Southern civilians in Georgia and the Carolinas was not significant in ending the war. It was, instead, as Sherman said, retribution for their supporting their menfolk in the Confederate army. It was immoral. Sheridan's impoverishment of farmers in Virginia was of a different type—it was to deny food supplies to the Confederate Army besieged in Petersburg. Destitution of the Southern civilian population in the Shenandoah Valley was unavoidable collateral damage.

British bombing of German cities and slaughter of population during World War II were primarily retribution for German attacks on British cities. British bombing likely killed more German civilians than did American bombing. The British had the excuse that Germany had bombed civilian targets in England, including the destruction of a million homes in London and the killing of some 30,000 civilians. Thus, the British argue that their attacks on German civilians were retaliation. The British response put the British on the same moral level as the Germans in this regard.

The U.S. had no such excuse. American civilian losses in the war were very small. There was no significant bombing of American civilian targets by Germany or Japan. Yet the United States attacked civilians in both countries, killing large numbers. The United States' bombing was for several reasons, including destruction of war-making capabilities. This is the reason the Americans bombed Germany in daylight rather than, like the British, at night. During daylight military-related targets could be more easily identified. But another purpose of the American bombing was terrorizing the civilian population of our adversaries into surrender. Terrorizing a civilian population into surrender was the notion of the advocates of strategic bombing during the period between the two world wars. It didn't work. In both Germany and Japan the civilian population endured great suffering and slaughter until their governments chose to surrender—in Germany because the country was being overrun by Allied troops; in Japan because the Emperor decided to stop the slaughter.

The American slaughter of German civilians by bombing during World War II provided little or no military advantage. There was, of course, bombing intended to destroy military targets; and there was collateral damage to civilians from this. But we also did heavy attacks directed at civilians. Some of our top military leaders recognized this, including Dwight Eisenhower, and were disturbed by the bombing of civilians. We lacked even the British justification of retaliation. The casualty lists for World War II show virtually no American civilian deaths from bombing. In the case of Japan, industrial production was often scattered in small units throughout Japanese cities. The military objective of destroying war production resulted in civilian casualties. (Incidentally, in the case of the atomic bomb dropped on Nagasaki, it has been argued that as much as one-third of those killed were military personnel or working in defense production. But eliminating defense production was not the primary purpose of the bombing, as we shall see below.)

There was bombing by Americans for the purpose of killing civilians. For example, the fire-bombing of Tokyo when some 70,000 people are said to have died in a few days, was primarily for the purpose of terrorizing the civilian population and as retaliation for

Japanese attacks on American military force. There had been and were few Japanese attacks on American civilians. For example, Pearl Harbor was an attack on our military; Honolulu's civilian population was not targeted. But we responded with the slaughter of Japanese civilians.

The two atomic attacks were, to a large degree, different. They were an effort to cause Japanese leaders to recognize that the wear was unwinnable and to therefore bring an end to the war. The alternative would have involved an Allied invasion of Japan which would have been bloody and destructive beyond even the bombs. The bombs were not an effort to terrorize the civilian population, though they did that, but rather to persuade the government. And, of course, they succeeded.

In modern times drone attacks often have civilian casualties associated with them. But they have not been intended to terrorize a civilian population. If they were so intended, they don't seem large enough in scope and impact to be likely to do so. Instead, at this point, civilian casualties associated with drone strikes seem largely unavoidable collateral damage. In the future, however, drones might be armed with weapons of mass destruction and become weapons used to terrorize civilian populations. This is most likely to occur in the midst of a large-scale war, like World War II or the Civil War, when American authorities are willing to target civilians on a large scale.

American governments do not always seek to terrorize civilian populations. This has not been done systematically in any American war since World War II. In fact, the official policy of the American government since World War II has been the opposite. The American military has sought to minimize civilian casualties in order to win the support, or at least the neutrality, of the civilian population. Yet, the heritage of the Civil War and World War II has made Americans generally less concerned about civilian casualties abroad than would otherwise be the case. In the second Iraqi war some 30,000 civilians are said to have died, many as collateral damage from American military action directed at Iraqi forces or terrorists. In the Afghanistan War some 15,000 civilians are said to have died as a consequence of American and allied military actions against the Taliban.

These numbers are dwarfed by the slaughter in World War II. Hundreds of thousands of Germans and perhaps a million or more Japanese civilians were killed by American bombing campaigns.

It's not even clear that Sherman's terrorizing the civilian population of Georgia and the Carolinas worked to end the Civil War. It was the approach of Sherman's army from the Carolinas which forced Lee to try to escape Grant's army, only to be surrounded and forced to surrender. If the misery of the civilian population of Georgia and the Carolina's affected the military situation at all, it would have to be through an unwillingness of Southern men to leave their homes defenseless while going to serve in the Confederate armies. It is possible, but not certain, that such reluctance played some role in the end of the war. Otherwise, Sherman's attack on the civilian population of the South was merely punitive and accomplished no strategic purpose at all.

What are the rationales offered for making war on civilians?

a. To win the war by making civilians suffer. This is the rationale offered for terror bombing which was tested and failed in Europe in WWII.

b. To save lives. This was rationale for dropping atomic bombs on Japan. In the unusual situation of World War II Japan, in which the emperor seized on the bombing as a reason for surrender, terror bombing may have ended up saving lives. But the circumstances were very unusual. Terror bombing directed at Germany had no such result.

c. To cut off supplies to an enemy army. Refugees and dead civilians cannot make weapons and cannot provide supplied to enemy military forces. Yet despite terror bombing, German production increased until Allied armies began to overrun Germany at the end of the Second World War.

d. To punish enemy civilians for their guilt in the war. This is a barbaric application of the doctrine of collective guilt.

e. Every country does it. Terror attacks on civilians are common. So we should do it, also. But the United States has done terror bombing on the largest scale in history (only the British come close), and this cannot be justified by pointing to much more limited actions by others.

None of the rationales for terrorizing civilians which are listed above are convincing; nor are they convincing as a group. The United States ought to stop terror attacks on civilians as an element of strategic warfare. Fortunately, we haven't done it in recent wars; but they have been much smaller than the Civil War and World War II, and the danger is that if another large-scale conflict occurs, we will revert to our pattern which began in the Civil War and reached it height in World War II.

It is the application of the doctrine of terror war by the United States to civilian populations of enemies that is gives some credibility to charges that America is a terrorist nation. To be sure, adversaries, government or non-governmental, often place civilians in harm's way in order to gain propaganda advantage. In the same way, adversaries sometimes use women and children to deliver bombs, again accepting civilian deaths.

PART FIVE

America Can Be Healed from the Civil War

CHAPTER ELEVEN

America Can Be Fully Unified

The long shadows of the Civil War should be lifted from America. In order for this to happen, the politics, economy and society of the United States must be purged of its residue from the Civil War. This has never been seriously attempted, but it can be done. The United States can be fully unified.

A Legacy of Division

The essence of the legacy of the American Civil War is division in our country. The war was an attempt by the South to divide the country. The attempt failed at one level, but the country was left divided by the war on many other levels.

What would an America that is healed from the Civil War look like? It would be a more homogenous country without sectional and demographic voting blocs. There would be less animosity between people by section and race.

An America healed from the Civil War would be an America truly reunited. There would not be sectional economic exploitation; there would not be excessive federal government intrusion and corruption; there would not be racism; there would not be de facto segregation; there would be candor among us about our motivations in international politics. These are the things that require correction.

The good things that came from the Civil War—political unity and an end to slavery—will, of course, be retained.

Though slavery has been gone from the United States for more than 150 years, it continues to exist in various forms in the world. Some 30 million of people are said to be held in slavery worldwide today. Many Americans ignore slavery elsewhere, but it exists and still has a large racial component.

Eliminating slavery everywhere in the modern world is unfinished business which is related to America's effort in the Civil War to end slavery at home. America's war against slavery at that time was part of a global effort to end slavery which was led by Christian churches in England and New England. But though slavery was ended at that time in America and much of the world, it was not ended everywhere. Ending slavery world-wide would complete the agenda of emancipation begun in the 19th century and should be a high priority item on our national agenda.

Escaping Racism

The Decline of Racism

There is evidence today that racism is declining. Many younger Americans believe that they are no longer racist at all. African-Americans seem to act as though the sectional distribution of racism is much less skewed than it used to be. There has been a substantial movement of African-Americans within the U.S. from central cities of the North to the big cities of the South. This is a partial reversal of the pattern of internal migration which in the first two-thirds of the 20th century took millions of African-Americans from rural areas of the South into the cities of the North. That African-Americans are returning to the South would seem to indicate that racism has declined in the South.

The emergence of African-American immigration to the South is strong evidence of a major reduction of racism and racist law and restrictions. Many large Southern cities are now governed by

African-American mayors and city councils, as is the case in many Northern cities.

The Reduction of Residential Segregation

There is recent evidence of a movement of African-Americans in many major metropolitan areas from city centers to surrounding suburbs. If this is a movement into suburbs that are becoming racially integrated, it is a step away from the ghettoization that accompanied the African-American migration to the northern and western cities in the 20th century. This would be a major advance toward equal working opportunity for African-Americans since jobs are more readily available from suburban locations. If enough African-Americans are able and permitted to relocate to integrated localities, then the subculture of the ghetto is likely to dissolve, allowing African-Americans to fully integrate into American life.

Doing More

There can be no end to the shadows of the Civil War until America escapes racism. The South must abandon its legacy of racism completely. It has made much progress, but isn't finished. The essence of abandoning the legacy of racism is to cease the quiet, non-public, generally tolerated racism that still occurs in white-society at all levels in the South.

The North must abandon its hypocrisy about race and end its exploitation of the racial issue for partisan political advantage—an advantage it has enjoyed since the Civil War. The essence of abandoning hypocrisy is to accept full residential integration. By ending ghettos and the culture of deprivation, the North will advance non-whites toward the full economic opportunity its politicians continually promise but never deliver. By this reform the North can finally begin to couple economic liberation for non-whites with the political liberation achieved by the war.

Ending Economic Exploitation

There is more to consigning the legacy of the Civil War to the dustbin of history than an end to racism. The economic underpinnings of the War require rectification also. The great banks of the Northeast should cease to exploit the rest of the country. As long as Wall Street exploits the rest of the country in its ordinary amoral manner, there can be no end of the sectional division that characterizes American politics. Today, unlike the Civil War period, the federal government, usually in the partisan control of the North, and always in the hidden control of banks, private equity funds and hedge funds, acts through its vastly expanded taxing and regulatory power as a new element in the exploitation of much of the country. This makes economic reform even more difficult.

Ending economic exploitation is likely to be much more difficult to achieve than an end of racism in the South and to racist hypocrisy in the North. When we turn to economic exploitation, we are addressing what the leaders do, not merely the masses. Leaders are far more clever in defense of their anti-social activities than people generally; leaders are also far more persistent and determined.

1. Economic reform

a. No economic exploitation. There has been and remains economic exploitation in America. Some people are encouraged by advertising and social pressure to consume, but lack jobs or incomes sufficient to permit the consumption and are encouraged to take on excessive debt. Whole sections have been deprived of job-producing industry for the benefit primarily of speculators and investors. Economic change and progress should not be halted but effective methods of adjustment should be provided for those adversely impacted, and motivations of exploitation should be eliminated. The financial services industry is highly concentrated geographically—in New York and in large cities nationwide. Most of its decision-making is in New York. If Wall Street cannot be reformed, then financial services should be more widely distributed around the country, so that each section would then have its own exploiters. Exploitation would continue, but its sectional impact would be reduced or eliminated.

b. The flow of resources from the rest of the nation into Washington, D.C. continues to increase. Throughout the Great Recession, Washington, D.C. boomed. When there was no construction in most of the country, tower cranes stood like chimneys on Washington building sites. Washington was notorious for corruption during and after the Civil War. But as the government shrank after the war, things improved. With the vast expansion of the federal government in recent decades, corruption (much of it now legal under our laws) has ballooned. Reform is not possible. Corruption is legalized rather than eliminated. Contributions made by special interests and their paid lobbyists to the campaigns of politicians are a scandal recognized world-wide. The Supreme Court of the United States seems to be endorsing the scandal repeatedly. Only by a substantial reduction in the size of the federal government can corruption be lessened and the country reconciled to its government. (In 2013 public approval of Congress sank to an all-time low of ten percent.)

Reforming Attitudes and Behaviors

More is required in reforming attitudes and behaviors than escaping racism, though that is the most important requirement.

In the arena of attitudes, Americans need to *rely more on reason and less on emotion.* Such an effort will reduce the likelihood of conflict, both domestically and internationally. It will help us avoid clashes based on prejudices reflecting races, religions, nationalities, genders and sections. All of these played major roles in the Civil War and were intensified in American life by the war.

We need to *avoid misrepresentation of the past.* It is not only the Civil War which is continually misrepresented. Americans would do well to study our own history more fully and to embrace more firmly its lessons.

We need to *admit real motives.* In private and public life we often misrepresent our motives. Politicians, seeking their own advancement, continually misrepresent their motives as being for the public good. They are not alone. Business people do the same. When our interactions begin with deception, not much good can be achieved.

We need to *acknowledge faults*. It is uncommon in American public life for people to admit faults. When admissions are made, they are usually of a spurious quality in which politicians ask for forgiveness for something they'd do again if they were certain they would not be discovered. The result of this behavior is that we don't come to grips with and correct real problems. A good example is the de facto residential segregation that continues in much of America.

We should *treat fellow Americans as extended family*, not as enemies or outsiders to be fleeced if possible. America is composed of a multitude of self-conscious groups —national, racial, religious, economic, political, etc. While we pretend that our politics is one of individual choices, the reality is quite different—group identification plays a major role in voting behavior. Some political participants and observers refer to this as "the politics of identification," and insist that recent presidential elections have been decided primarily on the basis of group identification. Group identification is almost invariably associated with prejudices against outsiders and the feeling that outsiders need not be treated as well as insiders. In a way, slavery was an extreme example of group identification in which many white Americans felt justified in treating members of a different group, African-American Americans, very differently than they treated others in their own group. The politics and society of identification are an extension, though not as terrible, of this same destructive attitude.

We should *reject ends as justification of means; and reject means as justification of ends*. These were the great moral failures of the Civil War period (slavery was, of course, a great moral failure for far longer than the Civil War period). Both continue daily in our political and legal systems. Justice and moral behavior require a balance of ends and means.

Reforming Society

- Racism should be eliminated in the United States, as should reverse racism, both of which now remain strongly entrenched despite progress on both.

- Residential segregation should be eliminated. This requires a change in public attitudes about race, economic position and residence.
- If racism and residential segregation were eliminated, African-Americans could be fully integrated into the social and economic life of the United States for the first time. Then African-Americans would be free to be fully Americans; fully individuals, not African-Americans first—as even President Barack Obama described himself, "I am an Afro-American," not "an American."

Reforming Our Politics

- Political reform requires the election of experienced leaders; people who are not just clever and inspirational, but knowledgeable and wise. Lincoln was an unusual combination of personality characteristics. He had little experience that would suit him for the presidency, but he had great human wisdom. It was his greatness of spirit which has endeared him to the ages. We have not seen that combination of traits in our presidents since.
- Political reform also requires keeping politics out of military and international policy decisions in the way done for a few decades after World War II. This does not mean freeing the military from civilian oversight and direction. It is a matter of degree. At the present, the military is used by civilian authorities for purposes for which the military is not intended or competent, just as it was used by the Union government during the Civil War. The most obvious misuse of the military in recent years is its assignments to nation-building in the Islamic world.
- Militarism should be rejected.

Is any of this possible?

Attachment to the Shadows

The shadows of the Civil War which we have addressed in this book are dysfunctional for American society. But almost all dysfunction creates some vested interest. So it is with the shadows of the Civil War. From these vested interests comes opposition to the actions that will erase the shadows. Racists oppose an end to racism and the further integration of our society. Politicians and political activists who exploit dependency and resentment will oppose, probably secretly, the end of racism and the further integration of American society. The makers and marketers of American public culture —in music, video and film—will resist the end of the ghettos and the sub-culture which they exploit for material and fashion. These people will covertly and surreptitiously defend de facto segregation, the culture of the ghetto, and economic dependency, all the while professing exactly the opposite intentions.

Devolution as an Alternative

If rectification of the continuing sectional division of the nation is not possible, then we might be able to accommodate ourselves to continuing division by resting more authority in the sections. That is, a form of devolution might come to America.

With the growth of separatist movements around the world, the U.S. Civil War can be seen in a different light. Perhaps the War was a predecessor to devolution of the type encountered now in the developed world—especially Europe and Canada. In Europe we see a trend of people insisting on their own geographical autonomy within broader political contexts. For example, within the European Union we see Czechs, Slovaks, Bosnians, Croats, Flemish, Catalans, Venetians, Scots and Welsh seeking their own parliaments and governments with powers. In the Middle East we see the Kurds carving out an autonomous section in Iraq. In Canada the French seek some degree of autonomy for Quebec. What is especially significant is that the demands of all these groups, whether the demands are met or not, are seen as having a significant degree of legitimacy.

Perhaps in America the various sections will receive significant powers, now that the states have lost almost all significance to the central government. The American sections might become like the small countries of Europe in which various peoples have some government of their own within the European Union. Perhaps it is time for the government of the United States to become less centralized in Washington.

CHAPTER TWELVE

America Can Be a Better Citizen of the World Community

Much of the world community sees America as hypocritical in its relations with other nations. To the extent that this perception is merited, it has its roots in the American Revolution and the Civil War. The Civil War ended slavery and the enormous hypocrisy—a nation devoted to liberty in which slavery was tolerated—which the Revolution had permitted to continue. But smaller hypocrisies such as racism and unmerited moral posturing continue to this day. A new America will end even those.

The U.S. has been viewed as a hypocrite in the world community from its inception. The Declaration of Independence proclaimed that "All men are created equal, and endowed..." But many of the signers owned slaves. At that time, the Constitution protected slavery. Additionally, the Bill of Rights didn't extend to slaves.

Ownership of slaves by Washington and Jefferson and other founding fathers has given rise to much complaint in recent years. It is common to read comments such as "by defending slavery many of the most prominent of the founding fathers betrayed their ideals of liberty. They made themselves shrill hypocrites." This is a classic application of modern attitudes to a different time period, something most historians caution against. Nonetheless, the condemnation is true so far as it goes. Slavery did make a mockery of a commitment to human equality and liberty.

It is common for Northerners today to castigate Southerners of the Revolutionary period who signed the Declaration of Independence for hypocrisy. But the same charge can be made with considerable justification against the Northerners who signed.

Further, the North continues to justify its military conquest of the South on the basis of the moral imperative to end slavery. But there were economic and political motivations as well. In fact, Lincoln insisted these were the sole motivations.

Stressing morality and denying economic and political motivations has continued in American policy and appears hypocritical to many observers abroad.

We continue a pattern of hypocrisy in many matters. For example, the United States complains about terror attacks which kill a few thousand civilians. Yet the United States is viewed abroad as the largest killer of civilians since the Mongols in the 13th century and the Islamic conquerors of India in the 15th century. Americans gained this reputation via our massive air attacks on German and Japanese population centers during the Second World War.

Americans don't like to be criticized and filter out criticisms made from abroad that are not politically useful at home. We do not publicize the continual criticism from abroad that describes our hypocrisy about certain things. For example, American politicians and media are expressing outrage that Assad of Syria would "kill his own people," and the number of dead is estimated at 9,000 or so. Assad responds that the people being killed are rebels. Are the American critics really upset that Assad is killing his own people?

Think of an American parallel. Abraham Lincoln was responsible for killing his own people. He insisted they were his own, and they insisted they weren't—that was, according to Lincoln, the heart of the controversy. Lincoln was prepared to kill them to compel them to remain in the Union, and thereby be his own people. Lincoln killed on a much more massive scale than the dictator of Syria—some 350,000 southerners, "rebels," were killed in a war that cost some 750,000 dead (the newest, best estimates) in total. But we Americans don't condemn Lincoln for killing his own people—not at all. Why don't we condemn Lincoln for killing his own people? Because we support his purpose. So it's not Assad's killing his own people that we really object to; it's that we agree with the rebels on other matters, and not with Assad. This dishonest posture of moral condemnation is seen abroad as American hypocrisy. We do it all the time.

Nonetheless, condemning hypocrisy can be taken too far. For example, the British politicians of the 17th and 18th centuries who in their conflicts with the Stuart kings established modern human rights—including, for example, the right of habeas corpus and the predominance of legislatures in government—did not extend these rights to Irish Catholics. These British politicians, the great makers of modern freedom were deficient in this, by modern standards, but are they thereby simply to be dismissed as hypocrites? Not at all. They were merely imperfect, as all of us are.

Similarly, the fact that many of America's founding fathers owned slaves and were hypocrites about their devotion to equality and liberty means no more than what it says. They were hypocrites about this matter. Hypocrisy does not extend to what they did in the cause of human freedom. Since we are all hypocrites to some degree, if we were to use hypocrisy as a standard for rejection of everything a person does, we'd be left with little to accept. That some of the Founding Fathers were hypocrites about some aspects of liberty—including the rights of women as well as of slaves—does not mean that the American Revolution should be cancelled and that the colonies should be given back to the British; nor does it mean that the Democratic Party (founded by Jefferson) should be abolished; nor does it mean that the Founding Fathers were not courageous and far-sighted in what they accomplished by creating the United States. In other words, the fact that many of the Founding Fathers owned slaves does not have the great political significance in the modern world that some of today's historians and commentators seem to think. To conclude otherwise is to throw the baby out with the bath water—to be willing to sacrifice the United States to a short-coming of some of its founders.

The same argument can be made with respect to much of what America does in the world. The fact that the country often appears hypocritical does not mean that all that it does in the world should be discounted. But it would be easier and more likely successful for the United States to press an agenda of human rights and human freedom abroad if America were less hypocritical in the process.

Americans Should Be Able to Act Openly for Geo-political Reasons

America, like all nations, does things for geo-political reasons. But America, unlike most nations, cannot admit to itself or to other nations that it does this. So American political leaders try to disguise America's geo-political motives. Many people in and out of the U.S. see this as nothing more than hypocrisy.

This strange tendency of American leaders has its origins in our Civil War. The Civil War was begun for geo-political reasons—to preserve the American Union. It was later rationalized as a moral crusade—to end slavery.

Lincoln could not have been more insistent at the outset of the war that he was acting only on Constitutional grounds—that he had a solemn obligation in his oath of office as President to preserve and defend the Constitution of the United States. This he interpreted to mean the preservation of the Union. He was equally clear about the role of slavery in his decision. Lincoln wrote to a major abolitionist in August, 1862, as follows: "My paramount object in this struggle is to save the Union, and is not either to save or to destroy slavery. If I could save the Union without freeing any slave I would do it, and if I could save it by freeing all the slaves I would do it; and if I could save it by freeing some and leaving others alone I would also do that. What I do about slavery, and the colored race, I do because I believe it helps to save the Union; and what I forbear, I forbear because I do not believe it would help to save the Union."

Lincoln was a very insightful attorney and made his Constitutional case for the use of force against the Southern states convincingly to much of the public of the North. For many of the elite of the North the convincing grounds for war were to preserve the economic and political advantages to the Northeast and Midwest of a united continent. These—constitutional, economic, and political—were geopolitical grounds. There were also emotional grounds—the attachment of Northerners to the federal union.

As discussed in a previous chapter, during the Civil War the effort and human cost to the North of compelling the South to stay in the Union rose so rapidly that Lincoln decided that a matter of politics (or geo-politics) alone was insufficient motivation to sustain the North's commitment. When the cost of the War became apparent in lives and treasure, political purposes and emotional attachment to the Union were not sufficient to mobilize support enough to win the war. A moral motivation became necessary. Hence Lincoln resorted to the issue of slavery. As the second year of warfare continued, Lincoln sought to put the war on a firmer motivational basis in the North by extending the motivation beyond preserving the Union. Therefore, he issued the Emancipation Proclamation—so that the war had a firm moral basis.

The abolition of slavery became the moral issue that mobilized continuing support for the enormous human cost of the war. This is the interpretation of events—including issuance of the Emancipation Proclamation—given by the most prominent of Northern historians of the War.

American politicians learned a lesson from this. The American public prefers to hide its real motivations from itself, preferring not to think deeply about matters and instead preferring to respond to surface level causes. Major wars require sacrifices that the American population will not make without the spur of a moral motivation. Thereafter, in our major wars our Presidents sought moral motivation. In World War I it was not enough to frustrate the geo-political ambitions of Germany, Austria and Turkey for larger empires. Instead, President Wilson asked Americans to fight "to make the world safe for democracy." This was to be done in alliance with the Czarist autocracy in Russia. In fact, when the Russian Revolution occurred, President Wilson sent a few thousand American soldiers to Russia to support the counter-revolutionary forces.

Prior to World War II President Franklin Roosevelt was unable to persuade his countrymen to frustrate the geo-political ambitions of Germany and Japan. It was only when the Japanese gave him a moral issue of the highest value by attacking the United States without warning that he was able to lead a country that was politically united into war.

Thus it became the usual (but not invariable) practice of the president to extend the lesson provided by Lincoln during the Civil War—to minimize or suppress the geo-political objectives of war and champion instead moral rationales for military action.

During the Vietnam War President Johnson failed to identify a convincing moral reason for the war and saw moral indignation turned against his war. Largely in consequence, he failed to win the war and win reelection.

The result is that by a process of presidential action and public opinion reinforcement much of the American nation will not pay blood for geo-political purposes; it despises such purposes and thinks they are evidence of immaturity.

What happened recently to the Obama Administration in the Syrian matter is that the Administration found itself engaged in traditional great power politics with Russia and Iran (and even China) in Syria. It decided it needed to do some things there in the traditional geo-political mode for the interests of the United States and its allies. But the Administration was on record that great power politics was outdated, juvenile, and passe. Secretary of State Hillary Clinton had made major speeches about this; so had President Obama. The Administration's Russian diplomatic "reset" was part of its well-publicized movement away from traditional geo-politics. The Administration had strong support for its position from its political base in the Democratic Party.

Following Lincoln's precedent almost a century and a half before, the Administration declined to explain its geo-political motivations in Syria candidly. It did not hide them; but it did not give them as the rationale for use of force against Syria. Instead, it resorted to the subterfuge of advancing a moral basis for its proposed action (such bases are never hard to find in this amoral world). During the Syrian conflict the Administration seized on the death of children from chemical weapons as a rationale for a threat of military action.

Unfortunately, America's adversaries have become aware of this predilection of American presidents and they have exploited the lack of candor of the American government in a variety of clever ways. In essence, it is difficult for a nation that aspires to remake the world in its own image to be unable to be candid about its geo-political motivations. This is another unfortunate shadow from our Civil War.

An America that has passed beyond the shadows of that long-past war will confront its own motivations honestly so that it can act in a timely fashion to forestall the need for major military conflicts. If we are going to be continually active on the world stage, we need to be able to do it at the proper times, and to do this we need to be able to be candid with ourselves about what we are doing and why. This is the real behavior of an adult. When we do not disguise our motivations but accept them, and get rid of motivations we cannot accept, then we will no longer be perceived as hypocrites in the world and no longer trap ourselves in the consequences of our own deceptions. Then the United States will truly have surmounted the racial hypocrisy which stained our Declaration of Independence and the motivational self-deception that shadowed our Civil War.

Moral Interpretations of Conflict Should Not Blind Us to Other Considerations

Focusing almost exclusively on the moral aspect of conflict is a mindset from which we haven't yet extracted ourselves. It distorts our comprehension of political crises today. Americans might want to be mature enough to admit real motives, including those of a geo-political nature.

Americans might also wish to be mature enough to not let a bad end prevent us from recognizing decent means. When our opponent is behaving bravely, we shouldn't vilify him. We should respect our adversaries when they exhibit noble qualities. Today, perhaps we might wish this broader range of mind to extend to our recent Afghan opponents. Afghan support of terrorism may be wrong, but it would seem that considerable courage, endurance and initiative have been expended in its pursuit.

America Should Not Demonize or Underestimate Its Enemies

A consequence of the American predilection for moral rationales for military conflict is that we tend to judge our adversaries on a moral basis. We condemn our adversaries as immoral, and vilify them. We are not alone in this—the English do the same. We normally recognize no nobility in our adversaries, if their objective is deemed wrong. We ignore bravery, courage, endurance, imagination, etc. This causes Americans to underestimate our opponents—both at home in political contests and abroad in international conflict.

Some Southerners fought for a bad cause with great nobility of character; some Northerners disgraced the noble cause of ending slavery by their actions. Many Southerners undermined the nobility exhibited by some of their compatriots by their own misdeeds; many Northerners redeemed the misbehavior of some of their compatriots by the courage and restraint of their own actions.

Robert E. Lee is a significant example. He was a great leader and a great military commander. He's often listed as one of the top generals of all time. He was a strategist, a tactician and an effective motivator. His troops were loyal to a fault. He was a modest man seeking to be where he could make the most contribution. He never sought command of all the Confederate armies; he never accepted a political office nor sought one. He could have become Commander in Chief of Confederate forces; he could have been elected President of the Confederacy. He didn't seek either; he turned both down. Had the South attained its independence, he might have become its president at some point. Lee's nobility of character is credited with helping continue the Southern war effort for as long as it survived.

During the American Civil War many Southerners fought nobly in defense of an ignoble objective—the defense of slavery. Ignobility in objective makes it easy to demonize opponents, but demonization can result in underestimating opponents. This occurred at the outset of the Civil War when Northern politicians underestimated the strength and resolve of the South and so urged Union armies to hurry on to disaster. It occurred again at the end of World War II when Americans demonized the German military and underestimated its resilience. The result was the Allied defeat at Arnhem and then the hard-won Allied victory at the Battle of the Bulge. The two battles delayed the Allied invasion of Germany and so allowed the Soviet Union to overrun much of eastern Germany. In this way, the two battles, which the American command thought beyond the capability of the Germans, contributed to the extension of the war by several months and to a major strengthening of the Soviet Union in post-war Europe.

CHAPTER THIRTEEN

What the Future Holds

Americans can step out of the shadows of our Civil War if we determine to do so. We can resolve the issues that the War has left to us if our leaders take us in the proper direction.

There are heartening suggestions of progress. Racism is declining as measured by opinion polls, by legislation that lessens institutionalized racism, and by improvements in social behavior which are visible to all of us. There is even economic progress, including the emergence of an African-American middle class.

Progress against the shadows of the Civil War is certainly the best response for our country. Continuing progress would allow the Civil War-induced fault line in our presidential politics to disappear. Racism would be gone; African-Americans would be fully integrated into our society, including broad-based economic achievement. This is the best result for America. If these things were accomplished, America would be a much better place.

Many Americans, perhaps most, would support initiatives to step out of the shadows of our Civil War. But the matters involved are so deeply imbedded in national politics that public leadership is necessary for them to be accomplished. National problems will not be resolved on a local basis.

Many times, however, we do not solve our problems, but merely leave them behind us. We move on to other problems that seem more pressing in the moment. Old problems are not resolved, but merely ignored; they fester, but without attention. As enough time passes, the problems recede until they are forgotten. They remain, but seem less important. In relation to other concerns, the old problems subside.

So it may be with the shadows of our Civil War. We may simply forget about the shadows of the war without ever resolving them. There is much evidence that this may happen.

Each new generation of Americans has less understanding of the legacy of the Civil War. We fail to recognize that aspects of our society are problems that have sources and possible solutions. Instead, they simply seem in the nature of things.

The demographics of America are changing rapidly. Many of our new citizens had nothing to do with the War—they were not Northerners or Southerners or slaves. They had no family members—no ancestors —who fought in the war or died in the war or were freed from slavery by the war or lost property and position due to the war. Americans from Latin America and from the Far East who have arrived in this country in the millions have no involvement of any nature in the War or its shadows. They are not interested in either.

America may be passing through the shadows of our Civil War and may never fully resolve the issues which the war has left for us. We may never fully abandon racism; we may never fully integrate our society; African Americans may never fully attain the economic achievements of other Americans.

But even if we do not resolve the domestic issues that are the residue of the War, we may want to compel ourselves to do something about our relationship with the rest of the world. We may want to reduce our hypocrisy; we may want to cease trying to remake other nations in our own image; we may want to abandon warfare against civilians in future great wars, should they occur, as we have been trying to abandon it in the smaller wars of the past three decades. These important things America can accomplish if American leadership wishes them done.

None of this requires America to cease to argue for and live out the values of a democratic society —including free and fair elections, an independent judiciary and rule of law, freedom of the media, protection of minorities, and religious and secular toleration. Setting an example is one the most important things we can do to further our better values in the world.

INDEX

ABOUT THE AUTHOR

D. Quinn Mills, an educator and thought leader, has taught at Harvard Business School and MIT's Sloan School of Management, and consults with major corporations and governments, and lectures on management, leadership, strategy, economics, and geopolitics. His most recent books include *The Leader's Guide to Past and Future* and, with Steven Rosefielde, *Democracy and Its Elected Enemies: American Political Capture and Economic Decline.*